Dr Hugh Faulkner was 74 years old when he was diagnosed as having cancer of the pancreas. He was given three months to live. As a last resort he turned to natural medicine and made a miraculous recovery. Today Hugh is 79 and feels as fit and healthy as he did in his youth.

'Against All Odds' tells his remarkable story and explores the methods used in his recovery, complete with recipes and practical healthcare suggestions.

AGAINST ALL ODDS

A Doctor's recovery from terminal cancer through healthy eating

Published by the Community Health Foundation
188 Old Street, London EC1V 9FR.

First published 1992

© The Community Health Foundation

ISBN 0 9518443 1 8

Made and printed in Great Britain by
Helios Graphics, London SE13 5AD.
Phototypeset in Century.

This book is sold subject to the condition that it shall not, by way of trade or otherwise, be lent, re-sold, hired out or otherwise circulated without the publisher's prior consent in any form of binding or cover other than that in which it is published and without a similar condition including this condition being imposed on the subsequent purchaser.

Text printed on 100% Recycled paper

AGAINST ALL ODDS

DR. HUGH FAULKNER

With Marian Faulkner, Simon Brown & Gioachino Allasia

A COMMUNITY HEALTH FOUNDATION PUBLICATION

CONTENTS

ACKNOWLEDGEMENTS

So many people have helped with this little book that it would be impossible to mention them all. Michio Kushi first suggested that we should write it. Gioachino Allasia was a source of inspiration and encouragement in the early stages, and has translated the Italian edition. We have had invaluable help from a whole number of macrobiotic and shiatsu practitioners. Hilary Totah who first introduced us to macrobiotics deserves a special place. Lastly Simon Brown and his fellow workers at the Community Health Foundation have gone to endless trouble to produce this book.

Hugh Faulkner

FOREWORD

by Michio Kushi

As we enter the final decade of the twentieth century, the world is poised at the threshold of a new era. The time is rapidly approaching when the dream of a planetary commonwealth based on health and peace can at last be realised.

The road to one peaceful world will not be easy, however, enormous problems need to be solved before we can enter this new era. Destruction of the natural environment continues day in and day out, while huge nuclear stockpiles still exist even in the era of glasnost and perestroika. The family, the most precious of human institutions, is on the verge of collapse, and in an age of unprecedented prosperity, millions of people don't have enough to eat.

At the heart of these global problems is a chronic decline in the health of modern humanity. The modern health crisis is far deeper than problems of inequality in the distribution of medical technology or the astronomical cost of modern medicine. The rise of modern degenerative diseases - especially cancer, heart and cardiovascular disorders, mental illness, and more recently, AIDS and immune deficiencies - has occurred even as medical science and technology have continued to develop. In fact the appearance of these conditions seems to parallel the spread of our modern way of life, including the modern diet, around the world.

When I came to the United States more than forty years ago, cancer affected about one person in seven. At the turn of the century, when agriculture was largely organic and food was still traditional and natural, it affected only one in twenty-five. Now, in the age of high fat, highly refined foods, microwave cooking, and chemical agriculture, one out of three people will develop it. Through the 1990's, over a million new cases of cancer can be expected in the United States every year, and the number keeps increasing. If this trend is not reversed, by the year 2000, every other person may eventually develop cancer.

As a result of these statistics, and of the individual suffering caused by cancer, people everywhere are seeking new approaches to prevention. Current research linking cancer to diet and other life-style habits seems to indicate that the disease does not strike at random but results largely from our day to day actions, including, perhaps most importantly, our choice of foods.

Evidence linking the modern diet with cancer continues to mount. In 1977 the United States Senate reviewed the evidence and issued a landmark report entitled, "Dietary Goals for the United States," in which six of the ten leading causes of death in the U.S.A. - including several of the most common cancers - were linked to the modern diet. The Senate Committee suggested that dietary change - especially increasing the intake of complex carbohydrates, such as whole cereal grains, beans and fresh local vegetables, and reducing consumption of saturated fat, cholesterol, and refined sugar - could lower the risk of cancer and other chronic diseases. These recommendations parallel the nutritional guidelines of macrobiotics.

Similar conclusions were presented in the National Academy of Sciences' 1982 report, "Diet, Nutrition and Cancer," and in subsequent reports and dietary guidelines issued by the U.S. Surgeon General, the National Cancer Institute, the American Cancer Society, and other public health agencies in the United States, Western Europe, and throughout the world.

The key to preventing cancer could very well be in the kitchen. For over thirty years, my associates and I have presented a traditional approach to food and cooking that fulfils the preventive dietary guidelines of these public health agencies. This approach is known as "macrobiotics", from the ancient Greek word meaning "Long or Great Life". It is based on the use of whole cereal grains, beans and bean products, fresh local vegetables, sea vegetables, and other whole natural foods.

The macrobiotic way of eating, which is low in fat, cholesterol, chemical additives, and high in complex carbohydrates and fibre, has successfully - and enjoyably - been adopted by hundreds of thousands of people in dozens of countries, from the Soviet Union to Saudi Arabia, from Thailand to Argentina, and from Britain to Australia. In North America and Europe, more than 15,000 natural food stores and co-operatives now offer high quality macrobiotic staples to an ever expanding number of people, while a network of over 500 macrobiotic educational centres offers guidance to people in many countries around the world. At the United Nations in New York, an international macrobiotic society has been formed to offer this way of life as a solution to problems of world health and peace.

Today, a worldwide consensus is building that a naturally balanced diet along the lines of macrobiotics could help everyone lower their risk of cancer. As I point out in the book "The Cancer Prevention Diet", whole grains, the staple in macrobiotic kitchens, contain beneficial fibre which lowers the risk of colon and other digestive cancers. In a study conducted in Japan, miso, a traditional seasoning for soups and other dishes, was shown to reduce the incidence of stomach cancer, while other studies have shown that sea vegetables, also a part of the macrobiotic diet, inhibit the development of tumors. Moreover, orange, yellow and green leafy vegetables, such as squash, carrots and others containing betacarotene, have also been shown to reduce cancer risk.

Not only is evidence accumulating that diet can prevent cancer, but evidence is now emerging that a macrobiotically balanced diet may have a positive influence on the outcome of already existing cancers. In a Tulane University survey of 24 patients with pancreatic cancer who began macrobiotics, 54% were found to be alive at the end of one year, compared with a national tumor registry rate of 10%. The researchers who conducted the study called the results "highly statistically significant." Further studies are of course necessary, and the Kushi Institute would be happy to co-operate with medical organizations in conducting research into the potential benefits of the macrobiotic way of life.

Over the years, I have met many exceptional cancer patients who began the macrobiotic way of life, overcame the odds, and went on to lead normal, healthy and productive lives. Dr. Hugh Faulkner, a former London doctor now living in Italy, is an outstanding example. Dr. Faulkner was originally diagnosed with cancer of the pancreas. Being a doctor, he was aware that medically there was little hope of recovering from his illness, and that the usual time of survival after diagnosis of pancreatic cancer was two to four months.

I first met Dr. Faulkner and his lovely wife Marian in 1987, somewhat coincidentally, at a seminar I was giving for physicians in France. I was impressed by his strong native constitution, his clear understanding, and his dedication and compassion for others. These factors, together with Marian's love and devotion to her husband, made me hopeful about the possibility of recovery. I explained to the Faulkners that the macrobiotic way of life was not a treatment or a therapy, but a common sense approach to living and eating in harmony with nature. They both understood and together embarked on the adventure of a new way of life, with a very happy outcome.

Dr. Faulkner's story is told with clarity, humour, and passion. It offers hope and inspiration to everyone, and can serve as a bridge between modern medicine and the traditional way of life represented by macrobiotics. It advances the development of a medicine for humanity that can turn our modern world crisis toward an age of global health and peace.

The dream of a healthy and fulfilling life belongs to every one. It is my hope that Dr. Faulkner's book will help people in every part of the globe realize this dream, and bring humanity one step closer to one peaceful world.

Michio Kushi
Boston. 1990

INTRODUCTION

by Dr Hugh Faulkner

The first part of this book is the story of my attempts to escape from a death sentence, together with the reactions of my wife Marian, who has played a vital role. We offer no magic cure, no panacea for all the ills of mankind. Under the threat of death, I changed my diet and my life-style completely - and to a great extent my ways of thinking. Has this cured my cancer? I don't know. Is this new lease of life - more energy and more ideas - due to macrobiotics? Again I can't prove it scientifically. Certainly I cannot guarantee that others with cancer can repeat my experiment. Yet I have learned enough from my own experience and from reading and discussions on macrobiotics and traditional Japanese medicine to realise that Western medicine can learn a great deal from these disciplines.

Because I have been a general practitioner for many years and Marian a nurse, we have inevitably looked at macrobiotics on the basis of our professional training and experience. I have not abandoned the orthodox Western medicine I was taught at medical school fifty years ago. The spectacular advances in the diagnosis and treatment of disease have clearly helped many thousands of people throughout the world. Yet the cartesian newtonian concepts on which Western medical science is based have left many gaps - especially in the field of prevention of disease and the promotion of health. Undoubtedly Western medicine will continue to demand proof that complementary medicine is effective and we see this demand as entirely reasonable. The constructive dialogue developing between orthodox medicine and the alternative scene must be encouraged and extended.

My colleagues in macrobiotics should continue to question everything - including their own most cherished beliefs. In this they will find allies amongst doctors and other health workers, and in the universities and the research institutes. Medical scientists are not all blinkered reactionaries waiting to pounce on the unorthodox - we all know only too well that no one has the monopoly of wisdom and truth.

I believe that macrobiotics can help many people suffering from cancer. When patients consult me I tell them the facts as I see them. I advise them to talk to their own doctor before embarking on macrobiotics, hoping they will find the open-mindedness and encouragement I have had from my own doctors at the Whittington Hospital in London. Some patients, faced with the realisation that orthodox medicine has little to offer, may feel as I did - that they have nothing to lose in trying.

In the second part of the book I have tried to describe the macrobiotic movement today as I see it as a relative newcomer, something of its history and more important, its potential. In addition to its direct role in the field of health, we believe that it can play an important part in the ecology movement, and the preservation of our planet.

In macrobiotics I am a student, not a teacher. I am therefore very pleased that Gioachino Allasia, Simon Brown and Bob Lloyd have told us in their own words something of what macrobiotics means to them. This does not mean that I necessarily accept all Simon's physiological explanations, but I am convinced that much of our orthodox medicine needs revising in the light of recent scientific research.

For example the first press reports of the discoveries which recently gave Erwin Neher and Bert Sakman the Nobel Prize for medicine suggest that they could help explain acupuncture and shiatsu scientifically.

Lastly I am very grateful to the Community Health Foundation for publishing our book, and to Simon and all his colleagues who have worked so hard to make it a reality.

Hugh Faulkner
Greve in Chianti
Florence, Italy

Chapter 1

The Story.

by Dr Hugh Faulkner

"The doctors tell me that all they have to do now is to find out what the body knows that they don't know and then the stuff will be easy to manage."

From James Thurber's last published letter (July, 1961)
Selected Letters of James Thurber - Penguin 1984.

Told by:- Hugh Faulkner: patient and doctor.
Marian Faulkner: wife and nurse.
Gioachino Allasia : Shiatsu practitioner and friend

Hugh: The radiologist seemed rather bored with yet another routine ultrasound scan - probably unnecessary. Suddenly he stopped and concentrated on one area of my abdomen. He didn't tell me what he had found but got up and left the room. When he came back he asked me to go back and see my doctor immediately. We learned from the doctor that the radiologist had seen a mass in the region of my pancreas, almost certainly cancer. He arranged for me to see the surgeon the next day. The surgeon advised immediate operation. When Marian asked him what would happen if I didn't have the operation he said that I would almost certainly obstruct. In effect, the tumour would grow and eventually block the digestive system and flow of bile. Indeed he was surprised that I had not obstructed already.

I knew that I could expect to live only a few months, with or without the operation. Cancer of the pancreas frequently presents with few if any signs or symptoms and is therefore only diagnosed late. No one can reach the age of 74 without accepting the fact that he or she is not immortal. But a death sentence still comes as a profound shock. In a medical journal I read about an American series of cases where the average survival time after diagnosis was between two and seven months. Few patients survived longer than a year and very few longer than two years. Less than 6% of all cases survived more than five years. Although it seemed unlikely that the tumour would prove to be operable, with the threat of possible obstruction we decided to take the surgeon's advice and go ahead with the operation.

The ultrasound investigation was carried out at the Whittington Hospital, in North London, on January 30, 1987 - the day before we had planned to return home to Italy by car. I had had some intestinal problems for some years but previous investigations had revealed no obvious organic cause, and I was clearly a candidate for the diagnosis of "irritable bowel syndrome", often used by doctors as a convenient label for intestinal complaints they don't understand. I had almost convinced myself that my troubles were psychogenic. Almost, but not entirely, because I was happier than I had ever been and had no obvious reason for stress or anxiety.

I had retired at the age of sixty-four after nearly thirty years in general practice in London. After a fairly straightforward divorce I had married Marian, a nurse with whom I had worked for twenty years. Just before the property boom in Tuscany, almost by chance, I had found a ruined peasant farmhouse in Chianti at a price I could just afford. It nestles on a mountainside, some two thousand feet above sea level, with breathtaking views of wooded hills and distant mountains. After fifteen years we still never tire of the continual changing patterns of mist and light and shade.

The ultrasound examination that revealed my cancer was almost an afterthought. A colleague was worried by my loss of weight and, despite the fact that previous tests had revealed no abnormality, persuaded me to consult the gastro-enterological unit at the Whittington Hospital in

London. Once again routine examination and tests revealed no abnormality, and my physician, Dr. Beck, ordered the ultrasound because an observant radiologist had spotted a possible filling defect in my barium enema.

The operation was performed on February 3, 1987. We spent the previous weekend informing our nearest and dearest. We wanted the family and close friends to hear the news from us personally - however grim. John Cochrane, my surgeon, performed the operation himself. He found a tumour - "the size of a cricket ball" - in the head of the pancreas. He took a specimen for biopsy which subsequently proved histologically to be an adenocarcinoma, a type of cancer. He decided that it was not practicable to attempt to remove the tumour, and performed a double by-pass to reduce the risk of future obstruction.

I remember very little of the early days after the operation. Whenever I woke up Marian seemed to be beside my bed, which was an enormous comfort. The ward was old and full, and short of nurses. It contained both medical and surgical patients, some very ill.

Marian: Looking back, my immediate reactions to the news that Hugh had cancer of the pancreas were rather negative. I was afraid he might even die during the operation or soon after. I prepared myself for the worst, reminded myself of the many wonderful years we had had together and felt very grateful for them. Then I wondered if I had taken in all the facts correctly. It is not always easy to understand what specialists say, even for nurses. They probably think we know a lot more than we actually do. When something serious crops up I want to be told the facts slowly, so that I can take them in in my own time. I think this is true for many people; they can't fully grasp the situation. Even if they understand the words, they can't yet accept them emotionally. At first it is all rather a shock and almost exiting, but most of us need time to go over things again and again.

There were questions I would have liked to ask the doctors - such as, "what quality of life can Hugh expect during these last few months?" - but I held back thinking that it was not the right moment, that I should wait for a time when the doctors were less busy. Also I needed to think out and prepare my questions so as not to waste their valuable time.

The hospital specialists gave us virtually no hope. I accepted the fact that little time was left. It seemed that the only thing to do was to try to make the last few weeks or months as happy and comfortable as possible. I didn't really want Hugh to go on living if he was very ill, in pain or unhappy. I've known people who still want to live even when they are in great pain and misery. I expect they hope that things will improve. I was scared stiff that this period in Hugh's life could be just horrible.

Hugh: After the operation I lost about ten kilos of weight. Marian tells me that I presented a picture of terminal illness to my visitors from my hospital bed. I was blissfully unaware of this. However, as she says, we began to prepare for my unexpectedly imminent death. While I was still in hospital we both agreed on the fundamentals. No concealment was feasible or desirable. All concerned should be told the facts as we knew them as soon as possible. Once discharged from hospital, I should inform myself fully on the prognosis and any possible treatment, though we already knew that orthodox medicine had little to offer.

I had already told Marian that if I had an incapacitating terminal illness I would prefer to be in a hospital or a hospice where my basic physical care could be carried out, hopefully by professionals who had chosen to work with the terminally ill, and who would be generous with analgesics and sedatives. I have always greatly admired the pioneering work of Cicely Saunders in the hospice movement and have known of those who have died in peace and dignity in one of her homes. Of course as a general practitioner I had always respected the expressed desire of patients to die in their own beds, but had too often seen this throw an enormous burden on the spouse or other relatives or friends. Personally I would much prefer to maintain my dignity and coherence as long as possible with my family and friends during what would hopefully be long visiting hours, whatever trials and tribulations incontinence and general loss of autonomy might bring. Moreover Marian and other visitors could bring in a breath of fresh air from outside and not be ground down by sleepless nights in a losing battle.

So we decided to find out about hospices and had excellent reports of Edenhall in Hampstead. After my discharge from hospital I telephoned this hospice, explained the situation, and was told that I would be accepted at any time we chose. This gave us some sense of security in unknown territory. At least I had the possibility of dying with some dignity as conveniently as possible. It did not seem at all negative or defeatist at the time. I had heard that Edenhall had some kind of religious basis, but when I told them that I subscribed to no church or religious faith was assured that this would make no difference.

Marian: Hugh really felt it would be better for us both if he could be looked after in Edenhall when it came towards the end of his life. I, like most people, wanted to be close to my husband when I thought he needed me most. I wanted to do the necessary nursing or caring, and felt that this was really my role. However I could fully understand his point of view and would naturally respect his wishes. He would so much prefer to have me visit him looking refreshed, with outside news to discuss and time to sit and be with him. If I could do this and give him encouragement and help during these visits, he would have something to look forward to. We had also heard about domicilliary care for the terminally ill and were prepared to find out more about it later on. Now this all seems so long ago, and we have put it at the back of our minds - at least for the moment.

While Hugh was still in hospital recovering from the operation I worried about his children and grandchildren. Should they see him looking so very ill? What if he's actually dying? Should this be their last memory of him? Is he well enough to decide when he wants to see the family or should I decide for him? We had had such a positive and happy life together that in spite of the natural grief and upset at losing him, I was comforted by the thought that I would have relatives and friends near me, and a background of theosophical teachings which I hoped would enable me to face my life with a certain degree of calm and wisdom. I had so much to be grateful for but I had the constant worry that Hugh was almost certainly bound to suffer.

We had of course discussed the possibility of Hugh dying in Italy in our remote farmhouse or in the local understaffed hospital, but it seemed more sensible to be in London, nearer to our families. We were already known at the Whittington Hospital and Hugh had a place booked at the Edenhall hospice, so if it became necessary we would try to return to London.

From the beginning Hugh talked so positively about his imminent death. It appeared to be just another adventure for him. This was helpful to us all, and especially to those of our friends and family with chronic illness. They felt that they themselves could discuss their life and their own death more freely.

Hugh: We had spent most of our savings and a lot of hard work in restoring our centuries old cottage in Italy. We had worked part time in the Italian National Health Service since its creation in 1978, and we had many Italian friends. But if I turned out to be at the bottom end of the averages and had only a short time to live, with secondaries and rapid deterioration, a remote and isolated farmhouse in Chianti was clearly not the most sensible place to be terminally ill in, however much we loved it.

Looking back at this period I was not consciously afraid of the act of dying, though I have a normal dislike of pain and suffering. The greatest threat was loss of autonomy. I had very seldom been ill, or taken pills or potions. As a doctor I was in a privileged position, both in my access to information and the speed with which my diagnosis had been acted upon. I was fortunate too in that it never occurred to me to give up, to wallow in self-pity or ask why this had to happen to me. In fact in this period after the operation we were kept busy trying to organise our remaining life together as well as could be, and had little time for introspection.

I had had no faith in a personal deity since my teens. My Christian pacifism did not survive the war in Spain and I had no doubts on the need to defeat fascism by military means, although as a doctor I was never called upon to be an active combatant. I have however immense faith in what George Bernard Shaw called the life force, and in the ability of nature to create an environment in which all living beings can survive, provided it is not ruthlessly destroyed by man for power and profit.

I believe too in the almost unlimited capacity of human beings for growth and change, once supplied with the basic needs of life. The frantic accumulation of wealth and consumer goods, whether by hard work or lucky gambling has never appealed to me. Often it seems to bring not happiness and contentment but fear and anxiety that you will lose all your gains. Despite the superficial attractions of consumerism and what has come to be known as Thatcherism, I believe it will become increasingly clear that it cannot resolve the basic problems of our society.

I feel no need for personal immortality, whether in an afterlife in a heaven, or subsequent lives on this earth. I am entirely content that the collection of organic matter which has been Hugh Faulkner should return to the common pool of life-giving constituents, that life should go on through my children and my children's children. This is all the immortality I need. However, this does not mean that I was reconciled to dying before I had expected. We were living in a beautiful place, our family had grown closer and more supportive because of my illness, and we had many plans for work and enjoyment still unfulfilled.

Marian: Then Adam Frankenberg came to see Hugh. The son of close friends, Adam was eight years old and suffers from neuro-fibromatosis. Hugh is like a grandfather to him, and both were concerned about death and talked about it. Adam and his sister Rebecca, who was five years old, and their parents Ronnie and Pauline, were a great comfort to us.

A friend asked me how I actually felt when we learned that Hugh had cancer of the pancreas and that there was nothing to be done. I had to say that I was not conscious of "feeling" very much more than I have described already. From the first moments we were busy trying to re-organise our lives. Perhaps I did not allow myself to give way to despair because I wanted to concentrate on helping Hugh all I could, on being positive about his rehabilitation from the operation and his remaining life.

Hugh: Even before any alternative had emerged, we had agreed that the quality of what life remained was more important than its duration. Whatever the cancer was up to, I decided to try to recover as far as possible from the operation. Many years ago I helped to start a rehabilitation and resettlement clinic at the Whittington Hospital together with the orthopaedic specialist, Ian Winchester. A small but enthusiastic physiotherapy department had co-operated fully, and most of the patients who needed it could get rehabilitation in the hospital or at a nearby day-centre, and where necessary, advice on re-employment.

While I was still in the hospital a young physiotherapist came to teach me respiratory exercises, but when she learned that I was a doctor she decided that I didn't need them! However I asked about post-operative rehabilitation and was firmly told that these days there was no time for such refinements.

We had previously bought a book on shiatsu by Yukiko Irwin and tried it on one another for neck and back ache and found it very helpful. Shiatsu combines therapeutic massage with the principles of acupuncture. By massaging acupressure points it is said that the flow of electromagnetic energy around the body, known as Chi in China, and as Ki in Japan, is enhanced. I found that it relieved pain and tension, and I thought it would be ideal for post-operative recovery. Therefore we decided to try and find someone to come and give me a shiatsu massage at home. We discussed the problem with my old friend Avis Hutt, a retired health visitor tutor who is helping us with our research on old people and whom I have known for more than 40 years. She rang the Marsden Hospital, the temple of orthodox cancer treatment, and rather surprisingly spoke to someone who suggested the Community Health Foundation. We only learned later that it is the home of macrobiotics in London.

I duly telephoned the Community Health Foundation as recommended, and spoke to Hilary Totah, who happened to come into the office at that moment. We discovered later that Hilary is a well known shiatsu practitioner, with a busy life of classes, seminars, conferences and private patients. She lives in the borough of Camden and agreed to come and give me shiatsu in my brother-in-law's house where I was still in bed, shortly after my discharge from hospital. The first treatment gave me immediate relief from pain and stiffness, and we booked further sessions at home and then at Hilary's house. As she was preparing to leave on the first occasion she said, "Of course you do know that Shiatsu doesn't cure cancer?" I said that we had never thought it could. She said, "But have you thought about macrobiotics? If you like I can arrange for you to see someone at the Community Health Foundation who will explain its role in the prevention and treatment of cancer." I said that I had never heard of macrobiotics, and would rather read about it before I met an enthusiastic practitioner. So Hilary provided me with a couple of books and Marian bought another from a local bookshop.

The macrobiotic books appeared to claim that health was the result of how we live our lives and in particular, what we eat. A diet of grains, such as brown rice, barley, millet and oats, fresh vegetables, dried beans, and a range of seasonings, condiments and other natural foods in moderation are recommended. The books also included information on a range of Japanese foods that were completely new to us. These included miso, shoyu, seaweeds, tofu and umeboshi plums. It was also clear that I would have to give up meat, dairy food and sugar. When I looked at all the macrobiotic books available I noticed that many were written by Michio Kushi, who I later learned has been instrumental in developing macrobiotics in the U.S.A. and also comes to Europe once or twice a year on lecture tours.

Here for the first time I read that macrobiotics believed that the body could be taught to reject cancer - in orthodox medical terms, that we could materially increase the slim chance of "spontaneous regression". Lying in bed I read all three books from cover to cover. It seemed that I had nothing to lose by giving the macrobiotic diet and way of life a trial. We discussed this with our families and friends and with my general practitioner, Don Grant, a very old friend and ex-partner. All agreed that since the tumour was inoperable and no chemotherapy or radiotherapy was known to be effective, orthodox western medicine offered no hope.

John Horder, another old friend and ex-colleague, thought that it would be useful to have an objective opinion on macrobiotics from someone outside its ranks, so we consulted Dr. Patrick Pietroni, a general practitioner who was the founder and first president of the British Holistic Medical Association. He assured us that the macrobiotic movement was completely respectable and sincere, but he warned us that he knew of no evidence other than anecdotal that the macrobiotic diet and way of life could cure an established cancer such as I had. When Marian asked him if he would try macrobiotics if he was in my position, Dr. Pietroni replied: "Probably not." Despite this rather lukewarm opinion we decided to go ahead. Macrobiotics appeared to offer the possibility of cure - however remote. Here Marian's enthusiasm and support were vital. She was far more ready to become a believer than I was. So we went to the Community Health Foundation and ate in their excellent macrobiotic restaurant, which is open for lunch and evening meals. We also bought more books at Genesis, the bookshop in the same building, and patronised Clearspring, the macrobiotic food-store next door.

Marian: I had no idea then that we could have such an appalling diagnosis followed by the five most exciting and happy years of our lives. One fascinating thing has been Hugh's attitude to complementary medicine and his readiness to meet completely new problems and challenges. Before working in our London health centre as a nurse, I had taken part in faith or spiritual healing with animals and later with people. I worked as an assistant to a well known healer. Later, I studied meditation, yoga, spiritualism and eastern philosophy. Then I became a theosophist and a vegetarian. So macrobiotics was not so new and strange for me as it was for Hugh, though he had encouraged his patients to try other forms of complementary medicine when he thought it could help or when they suggested it. Hugh accepted macrobiotics as a new challenge right from the start. The family and I were delighted by his energy and determination, and he soon looked so much better that we began to believe a miracle was really happening.

Hugh: On March 5, 1987, a month after my operation, I saw Dr. Beck and Mr. Cochrane again at the Whittington Hospital. We told them of our decision to try the macrobiotic diet and way of life, and they immediately accepted this and agreed that I had nothing to lose. They asked me to continue with the pancreatic enzymes to replace any possible deficiency caused by the damage to the pancreas and to aid digestion. They asked me to come back and see them periodically to check my progress and the adequacy of the diet for normal requirements, though they could hardly have expected my visits to have continued for so long. Subsequently John Cochrane prescribed the hormone "tamoxifen" which has already been used in breast cancer with some success. Its use in pancreatic cancer is apparently based on the discovery of oestrogen receptors in the pancreas, and some uncontrolled studies on the effect of anti-oestrogens on patients with pancreatic cancer. A prospective multicentre double-blind randomised trial to study the effect of tamoxifen compared with a placebo by the Department of Surgery in the Haukeland University Hospital in Bergen should provide more accurate information on its possible use in pancreatic cancer. However I doubt if it has played an important role in my recovery - but who knows?

On Saturday, March 7, we had our first consultation with a macrobiotic counsellor. We had booked to see Jon Sandifer at the Community Health Foundation but he was delayed out of London and arranged for us to see Ed Esko instead. Ed turned out to be a delightful extrovert American. He saw us in the evening after he had been running a whole day's workshop, but gave us his whole attention. He had absolutely no doubt that I would recover! He gave us our first advice on the macrobiotic diet and way of life, advised us to take cooking lessons, and strongly recommended that we see Michio Kushi while he was still in Europe. So we began private lessons with Caro Smith, who was then one of the cookery teachers at the CHF, in her small kitchen in Kentish Town. Caro is young and enthusiastic, loves cooking and teaching macrobiotic cookery, and we soon became friends. We had eight three hour sessions during which Caro demonstrated many of the basic procedures in macrobiotic cooking and we were able to take away the end-products for warming up at home. These individual lessons were clearly costly, but as there was no immediate cooking course available and we planned to return to Italy as soon as possible, this arrangement was ideal.

Like most people I was used to a diet of a little red meat, chicken, plenty of eggs, vegetables, white pasta, brown bread, regular use of sugar, chocolates, sweets and several cups of coffee a day. My initial macrobiotic diet consisted of pressure-cooked brown rice, sometimes with barley, or boiled millet, vegetables either steamed, boiled or stewed, beans cooked with vegetables until soft like a thick casserole or soup, and vegetable soups seasoned with wakame seaweed and miso, a thick salty paste. We also ate other seaweeds, and a salty sour pickled plum called umeboshi, tofu, wholewheat noodles, and stewed fruit twice a week. There was a wide range of seasonings and condiments. We drank mainly spring water or bancha tea which is brewed from twigs. I was advised not to have any meat, chicken, dairy food, eggs, sugar, alcohol, spices, biscuits, or refined foods. Surprisingly I was also not to have fish, bread of any kind or raw fruit.

Looking back I cannot claim that I found the transition to a macrobiotic diet very difficult. Cooking has been a hobby of mine for the past fifteen years or so, and from the first I saw the macrobiotic cuisine as a new and interesting challenge.

We had both decided that if we were going to follow a macrobiotic diet and way of life we should do so as seriously and completely as we could. This decision was clearly greatly influenced by my death sentence. If there was any possibility that macrobiotics could help my body to resist the cancer, I was determined to give it every chance to do so. In the early days I was far from convinced about this, and here Marian's determination and willingness to follow macrobiotic advice was enormously important. As she says, her experience with theosophy and spiritual healing allowed her to accept the teaching and philosophy of macrobiotics far more easily than I could.

As far as the actual diet is concerned, I was surprised how little I missed meat. I was however happy when Michio allowed me occasional fish. Not drinking coffee presented no problem, though most of us are accustomed to drink a lot of coffee in Italy, and I have drunk none for the past five years. We tend to have a few drinks during the day and although I like the taste of bancha tea I sometimes get bored with it and I don't like any of the grain coffees. Although herbal teas on the whole are not advised, most Italian bars serve chamomile tea which is acceptable in our diet, is non-aromatic, and I quite like it with a slither of lemon and no sugar. I usually drink this when my Italian friends are having an "espresso" or a "cappuccino", though we usually carry bancha or kukicha tea with us wherever we go.

After a lifetime of addiction sugar has been more difficult to give up. Mostly I use a malt sweetener, or more recently occasional fructose in powder form, though it is not approved in macrobiotic circles, and not always available locally. In the first year Michio's embargo on anything baked produced some problems. We tend to eat a lot of bread in Italy. I probably eat more wholemeal bread than I should, and we are trying to cut it down. Unfortunately the nightshade family, which Michio strongly disapproves of, includes some of the commonest found vegetables in Tuscany. We do grow some potatoes and tomatoes nowadays for guests and sometimes eat them ourselves - apparently without ill effects. Looking back on the early days Caro Smith's enthusiasm and obvious enjoyment was enormously important and right from the start avoided any risk of macrobiotics becoming a grim battle with temptation. But probably the most important fact was that even after two or three weeks on the diet I began to feel much better and more energetic than I had for years.

Marian: I too enjoyed Caro's cookery classes, though cooking is not my favourite occupation. The first thing I learned which is very important is the need to chew each mouthful many, many times. Then I heard about the art of balanced meals. Next I discovered that only vegetables in season should be eaten. I found these sessions most useful as a general introduction to macrobiotics, and in giving me confidence to manage the meals when Hugh wanted a break from the kitchen. Normally he does all the cooking, with my occasional help. It's his hobby and relaxation. I usually do the shopping, cleaning, washing up and washing clothes and most of the gardening. So I shouldn't feel guilty when Hugh takes over the cooking! But I do sometimes.

On the whole I like the diet better than Hugh does. I'm quite happy with bland tastes and foods unsalted and unspiced. Hugh prefers food to taste stronger, and often feels the need to add soya sauce and some herbs and spices. Fresh ginger is very popular with us and also useful, and certainly adds a lot to the taste of dishes. Hugh is not so keen on under-cooked vegetables and doesn't like seaweed unless it is cooked with other things. I love seaweed and could eat it on its own any time. It is fortunate that we both like tofu (soya bean curd), and tempeh (fermented soya beans), and we love all pulses, especially lentils. We enjoy whole grains and usually start the day with porridge, adding seaweed in place of salt and varying the grain or using a mixture which can be wheat, barley, rye, buckwheat, millet, oats or quinoa. We eat a good deal of whole rice as this is a staple in the macrobiotic diet and we like vegetable soups with seaweed and mushrooms, often adding miso which is made by fermenting soya beans with sea salt with the addition of barley, wheat or rice.

Hugh: My son Tim, who is a radiologist in Norway, arrived and was naturally very concerned about me. Trained in orthodox Western medicine he accepted the official prognosis, and though he agreed with our decision to try macrobiotics he obviously regarded it as clutching at straws. When I look back at my diary for this period I realise how busy we were, meeting old friends who wanted to come to say goodbye, having cookery lessons, finding new friends in macrobiotics and buying books and provisions at the Community Health Foundation.

Clive Jenkins, then still joint general secretary of the trade union ASTMS (Association of Scientific Technological and Managerial Staff) - now merged into the MSF - (Managerial, Scientific and Financial Association) - found time to come and visit me on February 24, obviously to say good-bye. Clive is a very old friend of mine, and I was part-time medical secretary of ASTMS for some years. When later he heard news of my recovery, he sent me a telegram of congratulations from North Africa!

It is difficult to say now whether I would have meekly accepted the onset of terminal illness without the discovery of macrobiotics. In our decision to follow macrobiotic advice as completely as possible we were greatly helped by Marian's brother Peter Weiss and his wife Rosemarie. Peter came to visit me every day while I was in hospital and after my discharge they insisted that we use their small house in Kentish Town as an operational base. This involved commandeering their kitchen for several hours a day while we experimented with our early attempts at macrobiotic cooking.

In all this activity the most important single element was the sensation that I was regaining control of my own body and taking personal action which could possibly - however improbably from the point of view of orthodox medicine - help my body to overcome the cancer. Recent reports from the new speciality of psychoneuroimmunology appear to confirm the fact that we can overcome the passive acceptance of inevitable doom by offering patients hope - if not of cure at least the possibility of improving the quality of their remaining life.

When the National Health Service is fighting for its survival it seems ungrateful to criticize the hospital where I have had so much support and understanding from my two consultants, Eric Beck and John Cochrane. But surely a progressive gastro-enterology unit should have the services of a physiotherapist who could initiate post-operative rehabilitation, a dietician who could advise the patient, the family and the ward kitchen on diet, and a social worker to listen to special problems and give advice on how to cope at home. It seems that these things are not a priority today, even in centres of advanced technology.

With some difficulty we managed to book an appointment to see Michio Kushi in the south of France, on the way home to Italy. He was holding a conference on Macrobiotics in Bergerac, mainly for French doctors. We arrived to find the conference being held in a rather grand country hotel.

Our room looked out directly onto paddocks in which various imported animals were installed. We were separated from a large bison only by a single electric cable, which however appeared to keep him effectively contained. Here we heard Michio Kushi lecture for the first time. He has great charm and charisma, and discourages any attempts to make him a guru or some kind of saint. Aveline, his wife, gave cookery demonstrations. She is very small and delightful, in her sixties now, but looks far younger than her age. She told us she came from a peasant family in Japan. At home she was brought up on the traditional Japanese peasant diet that she teaches today, though the western way of life has brought many changes in Japan. Both Michio and Aveline have strong Japanese accents and at first we found it difficult to understand what they were saying, but it was a very good introduction to macrobiotics and we learned a lot.

I had my consultation with Michio. Rather to our surprise, Marian and I were not alone. With us were two students and Michio's secretary at the time, Donna, who took notes. I imagine we could have asked to see him on our own, but in the warm supportive atmosphere of macrobiotics it seemed quite natural and acceptable. Michio listened to my brief history - it was exactly two months since my diagnosis. He looked very carefully at my face and eyes, and examined my abdomen. I asked him if macrobiotics could cure my cancer. He said, "No, but your body can."

He then gave us a set of dietary instructions, which his assistant had modified as Michio talked about my particular diet in greater detail. Most of this can be found in Michio's book, "The Cancer Prevention Diet." (see book list). The diet basically consists of fifty to sixty per cent of whole rice or other whole grains, well cooked pulses, fresh lightly cooked green vegetables and some root vegetables in season, preferably local and organically grown. Simon Brown will be describing the diet in more detail later. On this first occasion there were further restrictions - no flour - so no bread, cakes, biscuits or pizza, in fact no baked foods at all to begin with; no animal products, no fish, no raw fruit, no salads, no spices, no tea, coffee or alcohol. Pamela Haines, the best selling novelist, who herself followed macrobiotics, called this the "No No" diet, because every time you ask Michio if you can eat or drink something, he says "No." Some of these restrictions were relaxed in later consultations. Michio also stressed the importance of chewing every mouthful very well, of regular exercise, fresh air, pure water, and weekly shiatsu massage.

Marian: I took the diet very seriously and determined to help Hugh to stick to it as strictly as possible. We do not always agree about it, and I tend to fuss, which naturally irritates him. But generally Hugh is far more relaxed than I am about the diet - and indeed about most things in life. However I try to shop wisely, always with the diet in mind, and Hugh enjoys cooking and eating most of the things I buy or grow.

Our guests usually like to sample our foods but we try to have available other non-macrobiotic foods as we do not wish to force our diet on others. There is no doubt that macrobiotic cooking takes longer and requires more concentration than ordinary cooking. We like to cook with love and eat with gratitude. We try not to cook in a hurry but of course we sometimes have to. This happens to everyone, and we have to find short cuts in preparing and cooking our meals.

Hugh: At the Bergerac conference we were all given a large file containing the Physician's Macrobiotic Studies Programme. Fifty five doctors and other health workers, mainly French, took part in the conference though the language spoken was English. We met some very interesting people including Dr. Ken Bailey, a World Health Organisation expert in traditional medicine who arrived by helicopter and gave a fascinating account of dietary problems in Africa.

Dr. Tony Haines, at that time medical adviser to the British Foreign Office, was there in a personal capacity. The directors of the macrobiotic centres of both France and Holland were also present. Kushi's son Lawrence, a qualified dietician, was there with his friend Bob Lerman, who was the director of the Clinical Nutrition Unit at the Boston University Medical Centre. We had some most interesting discussions on the diet and the possibilities of organising clinical trials. Larry told me that doctors in the States often refuse access to their patients' medical records. He gave me a book review from the New England Journal of Medicine, one of the most progressive of the orthodox medical journals, which I found most interesting. A Harvard professor, Arthur Kleinman, was reviewing a report on Chinese traditional medicine. The author, David Eisenberg, was apparently the first American medical student to visit China "under the auspices of the Committee on Scholarly Communication with the Peoples Republic of China of the National Academy of Science." I have not read the report but Kleinman's account of Eisenberg's description of the remarkable feats of the masters of "Ki Gong" (the manipulations of vital energy) whets the appetite for more. "These powerful adepts either teach patients to concentrate and strengthen their inner Ki in order to improve their health, or send Ki outward from their bodies to move objects, break slabs of rock, light electric bulbs, or provide anaesthesia... The author's enthusiasm and sensitivity are likely to win over even skeptics to the view that these are phenomena worthy of scientific research that may be medically important." We are entitled to ask why orthodox Western medicine relies only on the reports of one lone medical student, however enthusiastic and sensitive he may be. All in all we were greatly helped by this meeting and my consultation with Michio, and set off for Italy and our new life in a very positive spirit.

Marian: The diet and way of life seemed to help us both from the start. We felt very stimulated, and after those grim days in London it seemed like a miracle. Here was Hugh - still quite ill - not just hanging on but enthusiastically accepting macrobiotics as a new challenge. Our friends and relatives have given us so much understanding and love, and have come specially to help us through difficult times. Italian friends were prepared to come to London to see Hugh when we thought he was dying, and other friends have come to our home in Italy to help us. We were even offered nursing help, and the use of a flat in London. Fortunately we have always been most welcome guests with my two brothers who live in London, and we usually stay with them.

Hugh: In Italy everyone welcomed us back warmly though it took them some time to realise I was not yet tottering to the grave. It was a great joy to us both to get back to our house, even with a totally neglected garden. We have no problems with pure air to breathe and water from a deep well, which our friendly builders dug for us after we had consulted a local water diviner when we first came to live here. We get some physical exercise by working in the garden, where there is always wood to be cut, weeds and brambles and creepers to be cleared away, and compost to be managed. Then we resumed part-time work with our research group in the local health district.

By joining a local sports club we are able to use a championship swimming pool near our office in our lunch hour. Most days the pool is pleasantly warm even in mid-winter. This is important to me nowadays, because since I lost some of my superficial fat during my illness I am far more affected by cold. Amidst all the experts training with their fast crawls and butterfly strokes, Marian and I sedately swim the appropriate number of lengths with our slow dignified breast stroke. I even achieved twenty lengths some four months after my operation but this was unnecessary bravado, and normally I am satisfied with ten lengths while Marian does sixteen. We find this form of exercise, though rather expensive, extremely useful for keeping fit, and strongly recommend it. We also take part in a local authority old people's keep fit class twice a week in a school gymnasium near our office. For this we pay sixty thousand lire a season, rather less than thirty pounds. All very good rehabilitation.

For the first year after Michio recommended the diet, we kept to it as closely as we could. In the summer of that year I had two sharp reminders that my body did not welcome departures from the diet. On the same day I was entertained at an old age pensioners' lunch, I was invited to the British

Consul's celebration of the Queen's birthday. The pensioners had heard about my diet and prepared for me a large dish of whole-grain rice and carrots, and watched me while I ate it! I unwisely helped it down with Chianti wine, the first alcohol I had drunk since my operation. Later, at the Queen's birthday garden party, I could see nothing on my macrobiotic diet and stupidly decided to sample the caviar and Aste Spumante. My stomach objected violently and uncontrollably to these insults in the middle of the party, fortunately in the open air. One of my medical colleagues kindly drove me home in my own car, and his wife picked him up later. I made an uneventful recovery - slightly wiser!

My older daughter Lyn and her husband and three year old son visited us, and we took a week's holiday to stay with them at Lake Trasimeno, near Perugia, where we have a caravan. I went for a swim in the lake which was rather too cold for comfort, although the Germans and Scandinavians and even Marian seemed to enjoy it. The next day I had a sore throat and a cold, perhaps as the result of the swim. I was due to go to a seminar in Rome on smoking, and I did not tell Marian that I was feeling slightly unwell for fear that she would discourage me from going to Rome. So I stayed two nights with a friend in Rome, who tried to provide a suitable diet for me. We went to a restaurant which claimed to provide macrobiotic food, but served nothing of the kind. Another highly recommended vegetarian restaurant had become Indian and non- vegetarian overnight. The seminar was badly organized and offered very little new material. By the time I arrived back at the lake by train, I was feeling very ill indeed. Marian says I was grey and shaky and seemed to become semi- conscious and she even considered getting me admitted to hospital. However she drove me home to bed, leaving the family for another few days at the lake. By the next day I had completely recovered. I can only assume that my auto-immune system was unable to cope with the cold swim, an upper respiratory infection and departures from my diet. I resolved then and there to avoid cold water and treat sore throats - and my diet - with greater respect.

In June 1987 I consulted Ferro Ledvinka, a macrobiotic counsellor in Florence and virtually the founder of macrobiotics in Tuscany, and perhaps in Italy. He lives near Florence with his English wife and family. I reported that I felt extremely fit and full of energy, and that as far as possible I had kept to the diet recommended by Michio Kushi. Marian was worried that I was eating too much fruit, bread and biscuits. I said that as long as I felt well and my weight was constant, the occasional lapses were unlikely to be doing any harm, and that anxiety about them could do more harm than good. Fortunately Ferro agreed with this, but advised me to continue to follow the main lines of the diet, at least until we saw Michio again. He also recommended weekly shiatsu so we fixed appointments with Gioachino Allasia, a shiatsu practitioner and macrobiotic counsellor who trained at the Kushi Institute in America, and who has become a close friend. The shiatsu sessions were definitely helpful, and Marian usually came to watch and learn. Gioachino also gave us many useful tips and advice on the macrobiotic way of life, and told us of his experiences, both in Italy and in the United States.

Gioachino Allasia: The meeting with Hugh and Marian has been one of the most significant events in my life. In a whole number of ways I have learned about living from them.

At the age of 79 Hugh faces life with an enthusiasm seldom found in the young. Though he rejects any belief in the spiritual world, he is in fact one of the most spiritual people I know. I am firmly convinced that one of the chief reasons for his recovery from an "incurable" illness is his deep faith in mankind and his respect for nature. Certainly the presence of a woman like Marian has played a vital role in Hugh's recovery.

My first contact with Hugh and Marian was in the spring of 1987. Hugh had begun the macrobiotic diet and way of life a few months previously and had come to consult Ferro Ledvinka, an experienced macrobiotic counsellor.

Ferro explained the diet which he thought had caused the cancer - excessive animal products, red meat, chicken, eggs and cheese. Ferro advised Hugh to avoid all animal products with the exception of occasional white fish, and warned him to avoid salted and dried foods, gassy drinks, tropical fruit or juices, refined sugar and baked food such as bread and biscuits. Hugh didn't seem worried by these restrictions but was more concerned at his loss of several kilos in weight since his operation. The fact that he is a doctor and traditionally worried about patients' loss of weight obviously didn't help. Ferro reassured him on this point and told him that his weight was well within normal limits for his height. Both he and Marian were fully prepared to follow the diet recommended by Michio Kushi and Ferro. They had both noticed a definite improvement in health since starting the diet.

After this first meeting Hugh came to me once or twice a week for shiatsu massage. Previously I had not treated many cancer patients. Those requesting shiatsu were shared between myself and Alessandro Constantini, a physiotherapist and associate teacher of shiatsu. Since he is much more experienced than I am he tends to take on the more severe cases, leaving me to deal with the less severe. In fact he began Hugh's treatment, but asked me to take over as he was too busy with other activities.

Before giving Hugh his first treatment I reminded myself to avoid heavy pressure when giving massage to a person of his age. Conscious of the responsibility I began to give Hugh shiatsu. We got on well from the start and I had a chance to improve my English. Marian came to all the sessions, watching and studying what I did with the aim of giving Hugh shiatsu herself at home. From the very beginning her quiet presence made me sense the strong bond between them. Her decision to follow Hugh's diet had undoubtedly improved her own health and she seemed to get younger every time we met.

Hugh's back and shoulders were very stiff, but his hips and legs were fairly mobile. After the usual initial problems he managed to let me help him to reach a good level of relaxation. His abdomen was very hot, especially in the pancreatic area, and my hands could feel the block causing a local spasm in the abdominal muscles. During the sessions I tried to vary the techniques I used as much as possible, concentrating on his main problems. My aim was to prevent the body from becoming too accustomed to the treatments, and to stimulate a positive reaction.

As time went by, Hugh's skin cleared, and the excessive salivation gradually stopped. In view of his rapid improvement I encouraged him to press on and not give up, offering advice on the various problems as they arose. Meanwhile in addition to the diet, Hugh was carrying out an intensive programme of physical activity, daily exercises, swimming, garden-work in their enchanting farmhouse in Chianti, and his work for the health district. I am convinced that these activities played an important role in Hugh's recovery. Indeed, Hugh's energy increased to the point where both Michio and Ferro advised him not to try to do too much, particularly in the heat of the summer.

Marian: We learned that macrobiotics is about the joy of living. We are responsible for our own lives. Exercise in what ever form should be a pleasure and not a grim duty. We were encouraged to sing a happy song every day, and to give thanks before eating; to be grateful even for our difficulties - we can learn a great deal from them.

Hugh: We were due to go to London again to see my hospital specialists in July 1987 and decided to attend the international macrobiotic camp at Lenk in Switzerland on our way. The camp was held on a beautiful site, in a large sports ground with residential hostel type accommodation, surrounded by mountains. It was apparently constructed by the Swiss army and normally used for training recruits. We slept in our camper amidst the trees in the car- park, probably illegally, but no one actually asked us to move. Macrobiotic cooks and volunteer helpers provided excellent meals in a central dining hall. A fairly densely packed programme of varying activities was available.

Participants came from several countries - many of them young. We met a number of people who were firmly convinced that macrobiotics had helped them to overcome a wide range of conditions, including cancer. At 6.00 a.m. each morning a group of us gazed up at the mountain peaks lit by the early morning sun as Jon Sandifer led us in *DO-IN* exercises. These are based on the exercises described by Simon Brown in his book "Vital Touch". I continue to practice them most mornings - if I have not gone to bed too late the night before, or if it is not too cold. Sometimes it is an effort to do them, but they are so helpful and stimulating that when I omit them I feel that the day has not started properly. I advise any of you interested to choose the exercises that suit you best, sometimes vary them according to whim or need, and not become too anxious or obsessional about them.

Marian: Feeling too lazy to do *DO-IN* I decided to join Gioachino's group where we learned chants from various countries. I used to think that all chanting was monotonous, but in fact many of the chants were surprisingly tuneful. During the camp one of the most wonderful things for me was watching Hugh's steady improvement in health and vitality, and his joy in taking part in so many activities. We joined in cookery classes and other seminars and I went with a group collecting edible wild plants in the mountains. We made several friends and Hugh was very popular, especially with the younger people. We both enjoyed the camp very much and I was reminded of long past theosophical camps. We also visited a heated pool in a local spa near Lenk. It had jets of hot water hitting your body at various points, which was very relaxing and good rehabilitation.

Hugh: I had a further consultation with Michio Kushi at Lenk. Michio's firm conviction that I was forty per cent cured was enormously encouraging and reassuring to us both. He asked me to see him again in about six months' time.

Gioachino Allasia: Towards the end of July Hugh and Marian decided to have a second consultation with Michio at the macrobiotic summer camp at Lenk. Hugh asked me to be present at the consultation. After examining Hugh by traditional Japanese methods - skin colour, pressure points, pulse, the palpation of the pancreatic area - Michio took his hand and said "Congratulations! Your tumour has decreased by at least 40%. At this rate in six months you will be completely cured." It was a dramatic moment and I saw Hugh's and Marian's eyes glisten with tears of joy. Michio said that Hugh's case must be recorded in the annals of so-called "macrobiotic miracles", and urged him to write his story together with Marian and myself. I am delighted to follow Michio's advice because for me he is a very great man.

Hugh: Perhaps the sessions that impressed me most at Lenk were Saul Goodman's seminars on positive thinking. He is a young extrovert American, director of the International School of Shiatsu, who succeeds in encouraging the maximum audience participation. In the first session he said, "Don't believe anything I tell you. Question everything. Don't believe anyone." Someone said, "Does this apply to Kushi too?" "Yes, of course," said Saul. "I'll tell him" said the questioner. "He knows" came back the answer. Saul began the second session by saying, "I want you all to write down what you want for Christmas, what you really want regardless of cost or feasibility." Soon after he asked us to write down what we didn't want. I learned later that this is a standard ploy in some humanist psychology systems in which various psychologists and communicators are evolving their perceptions of the world, of themselves, and their clients. This approach is of course not limited to macrobiotics, but fits in well with the positive thinking of oriental philosophy. We have met others in macrobiotic circles interested in neurolinguistic programming, one of the recent developments mentioned by Saul. However it was new to me then and came at an appropriate moment. I still have the notes I made. For the things I wanted for Christmas, I wrote:-

A word processor
A compact disc player
Complete recovery
To play the blues harp (the jazz harmonica)
To learn to do wood sculpture
Challenges of all kinds

What I didn't want included:-
A recurrence of my cancer
Illness or death of Marian
Loss of autonomy in illness or old age
Antiques, jewellery, fur coats
Fast cars

After the seminar I told Marian of my Christmas wishes. She said, "Well, if that's what you really want, why not? We can use what you call my savings. I'd much rather we used them together on things we can both enjoy than wait until you are dead." So of course this came to pass. In London we bought a word processor and are writing this book on it. We bought Hi-Fi equipment and are very much enjoying the reproduction provided by compact discs. Another new and unexpected development concerns the blues harp. I got Dave Michelson's name from the Musician's Union, the only harmonica teacher listed in London. He is a young man living amongst a confusion of harmonicas and other musical instruments in a newish housing estate in Islington, only a mile or so from the Community Health Foundation. He has a bed available for fellow musicians in need. I had expected some tips on how to make some of the exciting sounds the great blues harp players of the past achieved. In fact I was instructed in posture, breathing, listening and keeping rhythm - and urged to learn to read music. This was all closer to the teachings of *DO-IN* than my ideas of learning to play the blues. Dave proved to be the grandson of J. B. Priestley and his mother teaches music therapy for mental illness. We got on very well, though it took me some sessions to learn to bend a note, and my repertoire is still limited. Dave completely accepted my desire to learn to play the blues harp at the age of 75 and seemed to find it not at all odd.

Marian: It was an interesting experience for me to be in on one of Hugh's lessons with Dave. They obviously understood one another and Dave gave frequent examples of techniques in playing the blues harp. This was very beautiful as well as instructive. I really enjoyed the session, and the tea and chat afterwards.

Hugh: In London I also had shiatsu from Rex Lassalle, recommended by Jon Sandifer. Rex is a charming Trinidadian, who admits to a revolutionary past. He is a qualified osteopath, and his shiatsu technique was quite different from any other that I had experienced. It was much more aggressive and often painful, with a great emphasis on deep breathing. I found it very helpful and stimulating at this stage. Incidentally Rex has now fallen in love with Italy and is moving here. He will be an invaluable addition to the ranks of shiatsu teachers in Italy.

We met several old and new friends in London, often entertaining them at the macrobiotic restaurant in Old Street. One old friend was Oliver Gillie, an extremely well informed and open-minded health correspondent, now editor of the health section of the Independent. He was very interested in my story, and suggested that I write something for the paper, which I promised to think about. Subsequently he arranged for a journalist, Barbara Griggs, to come and interview me in Florence. She wrote an excellent article which was published in the Independent in July 1989 and then reprinted in the News of the World. These articles resulted in several thousand enquiries at the Community Health Foundation in London which was mentioned in the article, all entirely due to Oliver's initiative, for which we are deeply grateful. I have subsequently been interviewed by two Italian newspapers and have been approached with a view to appearing on Italian television.

But to continue our story in 1987. August 3rd was one of the few days I wrote up my diary. I am not a natural diarist, rushing to share my innermost hopes and fears with a little book, completing each day in orderly fashion. However for some reason on August 3rd I tried to do this. In spite of activity of various kinds, under the broad umbrella of macrobiotics, we were still attempting anything and everything that might possibly help to defeat the cancer. The report of a tamoxifen study from Sweden in a medical journal gave the average survival rate of controls as two and half to three months from the date of diagnosis. Obviously I got a great kick out of being very much alive six months after my diagnosis. Saul Goodman said, "Did you get cancer to show what a great guy you are?" Rex Lassalle says I am intellectualising too much. "Just be yourself. Be Hugh! Don't try to become someone else."

But I am also a doctor, an amateur epidemiologist and an active campaigner for health for the people. Are those of us who discover macrobiotics a special self-selected group? This and many other questions need more research and further dialogue between macrobiotics and Western medicine. I took part in a workshop for health workers in Western medicine and macrobiotics in Poland and hope that this is the first of many in Europe.

On August 9, 1987, we flew from Heathrow to Oslo, to spend two weeks in Laerdal with my son Tim and my daughter Jill and her three children. Tim had invited them to come from London during our visit and paid their fares so we could all be together. We were met at Oslo airport by our friends Dr. Dag Bruusgaard and his wife Erli, who took us back to their beautiful modern timber house by the sea. Dag is a general practitioner and lecturer in primary health care in Oslo and ex-president of the European General Practice Research Workshop of which I am a member. We rested with them until Tim came to fetch us in our VW which my daughter Jill had brought from England. Tim had arranged for us to have a nurse's bungalow in the hospital grounds, as his house was not only full of guests but also Polish workers carrying out its restoration. This arrangement was ideal as we could cook our macrobiotic food on our own in peace and quiet. We had a very pleasant fortnight there. One of our happy discoveries was that raspberries and red-currants grow wild along the footpaths in this area. I had previously had an ultrasound test in Florence that showed some shrinking of the tumour and liquification and during our visit Tim repeated the ultrasound in the well-equipped x-ray department in his small hospital. It showed further shrinking of the tumour and the liquification in the centre. According to Michio Kushi this dissolving process of the tumour is typical of someone who is getting better.

We returned through Germany and were glad to be home after a very eventful trip - still less than seven months after my operation. In September we organised a workshop on the loss of autonomy in old people as part of our research project. Bob Gann, the very enterprising librarian who started "Help for Health" in Southampton came, with his expenses paid by the British Council in Rome. Our good friend Paul Wallace, the director of the Helen Hamlyn unit for research on old people in London, also took part. The workshop was reasonably successful and well-attended, and I was pleased to find that I could take such events in my stride.

Albert Kushlick, another great friend who is a psychiatrist working in mental handicap research came to see us. He is firmly convinced of the value of positive thinking, affirmation and meditation, and says these have all helped him recover from several attacks of coronary thrombosis. He too has had to deal with threats of early death, and I found our discussions immensely helpful and encouraging. Although he had not adopted macrobiotics, much of his thinking about illness and handicap is very close to macrobiotic teaching and practice. He is a firm believer in people being responsible for their own health and playing an active part in their recovery.

At the end of March 1988 we set off again in our camper for England with our good friend Gigi Passerini, a general practitioner in Sondrio, North Italy. He is an excellent driver and did the major part of the driving which he enjoys. We carried out a fairly tightly packed study tour involving long sessions with doctors who are general practitioners in Birmingham, South Wales and Devon. Out of this will come we hope, a book for general practitioners in Italy, "A New Type of Doctor," mainly based on the book with the same title already published in Britain by Julian Tudor Hart, a general practitioner in Wales who is another very old friend. Once again I was pleased to find that I could concentrate for long hours without any ill effects. One of our general practitioner hosts was so impressed that he telephoned recently to ask advice about his partner's wife who has cancer of the breast with secondaries. I put her in touch with Jon Sandifer at the Community Health Foundation in London and very much hope she will be helped in the way I have been.

In London one of our friends lent us a flat which was a great help and avoided overcrowding Marian's brothers' houses, especially as Gigi was with us too. I saw my surgeon John Cochrane who was very impressed with my progress and a full blood examination proved to be entirely normal.

On our way back to Italy in April 1988 we stopped at Frankfurt where we had a further consultation with Michio Kushi. He had been lecturing in a large building called "Pueblo" which appeared to be a well patronised health and social club, with various health promoting activities, including squash courts. Michio examined me carefully and announced that in three months I would be cured. He again urged us to write this book, promised to write a foreword and gave us the names of publishers in the United States who might be prepared to publish it. He said I had no need of any further formal consultations, but advised me to continue with the diet and way of life, which I have done - with some minor modifications. During the summer of 1988, I began a course of Alexander postural rehabilitation. Some of our macrobiotic friends and counsellors had criticised my posture and Ferro Ledvinka recommended the Alexander technique. We discovered that Fran Robinson, an enthusiastic and excellent Alexander teacher from London, now living in Pontedera, came to Florence twice a week to see pupils. I managed to get taken on with some difficulty as she has more demands for tuition than she can satisfy. I had already known about the Alexander technique for many years and had sent patients in London to Dr. Wilfred Barlow, a well known Alexander teacher, who took over the leadership when the founder died. This brief account is based on information from Wilfred Barlow, Fran Robinson and an article by the Nobel prizewinner, Nikolaas Tinbergen, professor of animal behaviour in the University of Oxford.

Frederick Matthias Alexander was born in Tasmania in 1869 and died in London in 1955. As a young actor he suddenly lost his voice. After orthodox medical treatment had failed to cure him he became convinced that his problems were due to his posture and the misuse of his muscles. Without any scientific training or previous experience he cured himself. He observed that the majority of people stand, sit and move in an inefficient manner. And so, as Tinbergen says, he became a kind of missionary and set out to teach, first actors, and then a variety of people, how to regain the proper use of their muscles.

The technique is based on exceptionally sophisticated observation and touch. It involves careful assessment and then gentle manipulation of the whole muscular system, according to the needs of each pupil. The number of lessons needed varies, but Fran recommends at least twenty - two lessons a week for five weeks and then one lesson a week for nine or ten weeks. Fran says that in my case it may take longer as I don't do enough relaxing in between lessons. Alexander teachers and successful pupils are convinced that many forms of under-performance and even physical and mental disorders can be helped, often to a surprising extent, by teaching the body to use its muscles efficiently. Since I am determined not only to defeat my cancer but also to become as fit as possible for my age, it seemed reasonable to find out if the Alexander technique could help me. In fact I am convinced that it has played an important part in my rehabilitation.

Marian: Peter Hand, a sculptor, gives Hugh wood sculpture lessons in his house at Pontedera, and after the first few sessions Hugh was producing beautiful little bowls, and more recently a small statue. We are very pleased with these results, and intend to continue with our visits to Pontedera. While Hugh works with Peter, I go for walks and enjoy shopping at one of the better health stores in Tuscany.

Hugh: According to Michio Kushi I am now cured, since it is many more than three months since I saw him. My fitness and sense of well-being support this, but I would feel happier if I had some objective evidence acceptable to my orthodox medical training that my cancer is disappearing or at least inactive.

The diet and way of life seem to suit me, and Marian's enthusiasm, the approval of my family and friends and the open mindedness of my doctors have all helped. I cannot prove scientifically that the diet and the macrobiotic way of life have helped my body to reject the cancer - but no one can prove that they have not. I know too that a number of people have been praying for me, including members of my own family and the Australian Sisters of the Carmelite Order in Tavarnelle, a neighbouring commune in Chianti. I deeply appreciate the clean air and pure water, the warm sun, the peace and quiet of the Chianti countryside. In Chapter 4 I try to look at some of the possible factors involved in my recovery in more detail. John Cochrane, my surgeon, who brought his delightful family to see us two years ago, says that he doesn't know whether my recovery is due to macrobiotics or the will to live. I think both.

Marian: My hope and happiness increased rapidly as I watched Hugh's health improve. How important it is to have hope! I was reminded of Geoffrey De Purucker's book, "Wind of the Spirit" (see book list). I quote the following:- "As long as man has hope he does not despair. Weak or strong, it matters not; if his inner spirit, the spiritual being within him, teaches him something of hope, he not only will never despair, but he will become a builder, a constructor, a worker with the universe, because he will move forwards, and this is altruism."

We are fortunate in having macrobiotic food shops in Florence, plus another couple of health shops, and markets selling macrobiotic and vegetarian foods and supplies. I know there are others in many regions of Italy. Even our little town of Greve has a number of macrobiotic foods much to our delight.

In Great Britain there is a lot of interest in whole foods and vegetarian and vegan diets. Macrobiotics is still not so well known and some of those who have heard of it think it is only a Japanese diet because of the use of several Japanese dried foods such as shiitake mushrooms, seaweed, and bancha or kukicha tea. Staying in Camden, North London, we had no difficulty in obtaining macrobiotic produce at Clearspring Natural Grocer, in Old Street. We also found a wide range of wholefoods at the Bumblebee shops in Brecknock Road. It was good to see a number of supermarkets selling some of these foods, and of course there are many health stores in London and most towns in Britain. There are also a number of guest-houses prepared to cook the macrobiotic way and we found a useful guide at Genesis Books, "The Vegetarian Travel Guide 1991" (see book-list).

Someone new to macrobiotics needs plenty of time to examine all the products carefully - and read the small print. It does take longer to prepare the food thoughtfully and attractively, and cookery lessons are highly desirable if it is going to be prepared, cooked, served and eaten properly. The standard macrobiotic diet is for those of us who are fit. People with illnesses need to see a macrobiotic counsellor who will recommend the appropriate diet for their condition. Hugh and I kept to a restricted diet during the first two years after his diagnosis, and had regular consultations with macrobiotic counsellors.

Eating out was a problem at first, which we partly overcame by taking our own cooked food with us; but later, once we got to know a restaurant we would bring in our whole rice or spaghetti and ask them to cook it and to add their own vegetables and some fish when available. Most of our friends are prepared to cook for us once they understand the basic diet, and many even enjoy the food. Now we are less fussy about it all but still eat out mainly at the macrobiotic restaurant when we are in Florence.

Hugh: In April, 1989, I was invited to tell my story at the Church in the Market Place at Isolotto near to Florence. On a Sunday morning I spoke to thirty or forty people under the sheds of the market, and afterwards answered questions. The Church resulted from a decision by two left-wing worker priests to continue their mission after a dispute with their bishop led to their removal from their parish church. For many years it has met every Sunday, winter and summer in the open air, as far as I am concerned, inspiring its followers with a message far broader and more liberal than that of the official church. It was a privilege to be allowed to take part and I felt very much at home there.

In the autumn of 1989 I gave a seminar at the Community Health Foundation in London entitled "The Older the Bolder", at one of their Friday evening dinner lectures. This went well, and we subsequently ran a workshop with the same title with Jon Sandifer in December, 1990, which was reasonably well attended. When Michio Kushi was lecturing in Europe in 1989, he asked me to tell my story to some of the large audiences he attracted in Britain and Italy. Then he invited both of us to take part in the International Macrobiotic Summer Conference in August, 1990, at Amherst, near Boston, USA, with all our expenses paid.

We duly set off by plane to Boston where we were met at the airport and driven to Amherst. The conference was held in the campus of the University in the summer vacation. We slept in a students' dormitory in a room with two bunks. We had our meals in the refectory, prepared by a team of experienced macrobiotic cooks with Wendy Rubin as head chef, and with several volunteers. The keynote lecture was given by John Robbins, author of the best seller "Food for a New America" (see book-list). This was an excellent start to the conference.

There were several interesting seminars and lectures, and it was sometimes difficult to decide which to choose. We ourselves gave four seminars during the five days of the conference telling our story and taking part in round table discussions. For the first time Marian spoke in public. Her contributions to my story were much appreciated - there was even talk of having a session for wives, husbands or close friends of patients at future conferences.

We met many interesting people including Elaine Nussbaum whose own story about her recovery from cancer is very moving. (Elaine Nussbaum, "Recovery" see book-list), and Dr. Sherry Rogers, who is one of the pioneers of environmental medicine and a confirmed macrobiotic, (Sherry Rogers, "Tired or Toxic" - see book-list) who very kindly gave me a signed copy of her book.

It was a great pleasure to meet Michio and Aveline Kushi again, this time no longer as a patient. They invited us to a very pleasant luncheon party to raise funds for the new Kushi Institute in Becket, now under construction. We also met William Dufty, author of the famous book on sugar, translated in several languages, (William Dufty, "Sugar Blues" - see book-list); and Shizuko Yamamoto, who later gave me a most exciting shiatsu, in which she used not only her hands but also her bare feet! We met Shizuko again in New York, at the macrobiotic Centre which she founded. Here we gave a seminar at a dinner meeting which went very well.

At the beginning of November, 1990 we flew to Berlin to attend the European Macrobiotic Congress. This was an unforgettable occasion for a number of reasons. It was held in the film studios of UFA, where some of the famous German films of the thirties were made. It is now a kind of commune where a number of people - mostly young - live and work to promote peace and ecological issues. Our macrobiotic food which was excellent was brought from the macrobiotic restaurant and served by volunteers. It was very moving to be in Berlin only a year or so after the wall was demolished, and a group from our congress held a session of prayer and meditation for peace where several people trying to cross the wall had been shot. Here they also planted an oak tree in remembrance.

The congress was fascinating. Most of the participants were actively engaged in some form of macrobiotic activity. The majority came from Europe, including Eastern Europe. We divided up into committees or working parties to discuss various areas - such as political, nutritional, ecological. I joined the political group and was elected chairman. We chose to look at the congress itself and redefined its objectives and made some organisational proposals which were accepted by the congress. I describe the objectives in detail in Chapter 6. I was delighted to find many people had been thinking along similar lines to ourselves on the future of macrobiotics.

The story continues. It is now February 1991. We continue to follow the macrobiotic diet and way of life, though Marian still worries about what I consider to be minor deviations from the diet. For me Michio's instructions and the various cookery books provide a general guide and not a religious dogma to be followed grimly and precisely. I am convinced that fresh organically grown vegetables, free from pesticides and artificial fertilizers are highly desirable. When our own supplies are not sufficient, Marian has managed to find sources for these in and around Florence, though they cost quite a lot more than the normal commercially treated produce. Despite our frequent travels for lecturing, conference and family festivities, we hope to grow more of our own food in the future.

Our lives continue peacefully and happily - friends and family visit us, and we them. We still work part-time on our research project on old people, for which we seek additional funding. I am on the editorial board of our regional journal "Salute e Territorio" (Health and the Community), and also of our health district news sheet. We have worked on this book - still with a love/hate relationship with our word-processor, and when this is finished we plan another book on old people. We still swim two or three times a week, and also attend the local old people's keep fit class.

In January, almost exactly four years after my original diagnosis of cancer of the pancreas, I saw my hospital specialists, Eric Beck and John Cochrane. I have just had a letter from them saying how good it was to see me "looking so well and full of vigour." A full blood count confirmed that all is well, and the serum and red cell folate levels are super-normal - doubtless, as Dr. Beck says "reflecting the macrobiotic diet."

At this time I also had a C.A.T. scan which showed no evidence of secondaries, and a reduction in the size of the original tumour.

Although I know there is always the possibility that the cancer could return I no longer worry about it. I now feel free to live my life to the full, and enjoy my renewed health.

Chapter 2

WHAT IS MACROBIOTICS?

by Simon Brown

The word macrobiotics was first used in this context by George Ohsawa. He coined the word from the Greek words macro, meaning great, and bios, meaning life. He liked this word as the aim of macrobiotics is to live a great life. After all, we all have a number of years left to live and the question explored among people interested in macrobiotics is how to make the most of this time. Practically macrobiotics is the constructive use of diet, attitude and lifestyle to support the desire to live a long, healthy and productive life.

What has impressed me most about Hugh Faulkner's experience with macrobiotics is not only that he has outlived all the reasonable expectations, but also leads an amazingly full and adventurous life. He is so busy that I always find it hard to track him down.When I call he is either swimming, doing his Do- In exercises, in Florence working on a research project, travelling on holiday with his family, off on a lecture tour of Poland, writing books, or away attending a new seminar on health related concerns. Of course when I do reach him I know I can count on his valuable wisdom and enthusiasm with our own Community Health Foundation projects. All this is happening at the age of seventy nine years of age and five years since he was diagnosed with what is usually terminal cancer. To me this is a wonderful example of macrobiotics in action, someone who is able to live his life to the full and is actually living a great life.

A few years after I began eating macrobiotically I became very interested in its origin. Up until then I had accepted macrobiotics at face value simply because I felt so much better. However the origins of macrobiotics make an interesting story and are important in putting macrobiotics into perspective with everything else. The beginning of macrobiotics can be traced back to the Japanese author and philosopher George Ohsawa who in the early nineteen hundreds first used the word macrobiotics in this context. He had been greatly influenced by a Japanese doctor called Sagen Ishizuka. This army doctor was convinced that many of the serious health problems prevalent at that time in the eighteen seventies could be helped by careful attention to diet. He conducted many clinical trials and published two large volumes of his results. This approach was so popular that every day Doctor Ishizuka awoke to find a queue of people gathered in front of his home. When he died his funeral procession was said to have been followed by a line of people several miles long. Doctor Ishizuka basically advocated a simple traditional Japanese diet based on whole cereal grains, beans and vegetables.

George Ohsawa used this dietary advice to help himself recover from tuberculosis of the lung and colon as a young man in 1911. This experience inspired him to continue Doctor Ishizuka's work. George Ohsawa later travelled widely and began to develop what was a radical new way of looking at illness.His observations of nature and people led him to believe that many health problems were created when people lived an unnatural lifestyle and had lost the ability to take care of themselves. He not only wrote about the risks of what he considered an unnatural diet but also of the importance of people's attitude to life. To Ohsawa this meant that people feel in control of their life and are able to take the initiative to be healthy in mind, body, and spirit.

When beginning macrobiotics I found many of the simple images used to understand how food can create better health profound and helpful in gaining a clearer insight into what I was doing, and what to aim for. I later found out that most of these models were created by George Ohsawa. The most famous of these is Ohsawa's seven conditions of health. We often use them as a definition of health in macrobiotic education and they provide a clear measure of how you are now and what to aim for.

His conditions are:

VITALITY: Everything Ohsawa did he approached with great enthusiasm. He stated that when in good health people would have abundant energy from the time they woke up to when they fell asleep. This energy would be consistent and when needed people could draw on a deep reserve of energy. He is quoted as saying "If you are really healthy, you can overpower and chase away difficulties one after the other as a dog chases a rabbit", and "The bigger the difficulty the bigger the pleasure. This attitude is the sign of freedom from fatigue".

Think how your own energy is from day to day and at which times of the day you feel most tired? Do you for example feel tired or sleepy in the mid afternoon? Are you sluggish in the morning?

GOOD APPETITE: This is interpreted as not only having a good appetite for food where each person is completely satisfied with two or three meals a day, but also a good appetite for life. Ohsawa notes that in his definition of a good appetite anyone should feel content with a simple meal of brown rice or brown bread.

Ask yourself ; whether you need to eat between meals, whether you have cravings for foods you would prefer not to eat such as chocolate,whether your digestion is comfortable and free from bloating and pains, and whether you have a comfortable daily bowel movement.

A DEEP NIGHT'S SLEEP: Ohsawa considered a short deep sleep from which people awoke refreshed and ready for the next day to be ideal. Ohsawa states that "Your sleep is healthy if four to six hours of it satisfies you entirely".

See if you fall asleep quickly, get a full night's sleep, and wake up completely refreshed. Do you have to get up in the night? It is common for people to have to get up in the night to urinate and therefore interrupt part of their deep sleep when the body is repairing and rebuilding itself.

GOOD MEMORY: Ohsawa placed great value on memory. We use our memory to judge and make decisions for the future. "Human behaviour, if it is not to end in misfortune, depends on sound judgment. Sound judgment, in turn, depends on remembered experience."

How good is your memory? It is interesting to find out what you remember best. For some numbers are easy to remember for others it may be names, visual images like faces ,or events.

GOOD HUMOUR: A good sense of humour and the ability to make and keep lots of friends all contribute to this condition. Ohsawa thought that not only do emotions like anger, self pity, depression, worry, anxiety and irritability reduce our ability to make the most of life, but also that careful attention to diet and lifestyle would increase our ability to have more positive emotional feelings. He was particularly concerned that resentment and anger about the past would spoil the ability to enjoy the present.

Do you often suffer from emotions such as anger, anxiety or depression even though you cannot find any real reason? Think whether you can fully enjoy and participate in your work and with your family, or whether you hold back due to some resentment from the past. Good tests are a family Christmas, playing team sports, and to what extent you can commit yourself to your work even if it means other people succeed too.

CLARITY IN THINKING AND DOING: "Those people in good health should have the ability to think, judge and do with promptness and clarity". This reflects an alert, focussed mind that is able to concentrate and see things clearly. Ohsawa also included the ability to create a sense of order in anything you do.

Consider how you make decisions, whether you have a clear long term direction in your life, and if you are focussed on the present. Perhaps you find it hard to concentrate, are confused or worried about the future, or tend to be indecisive.

APPRECIATION. We are all dependent on the air we breathe, the water we drink, and the food we eat. Yet how much do we appreciate this simple every day sustenance. How much do we appreciate our families, friends, and colleagues? For Ohsawa the mood of justice expresses appreciation for everything. He includes a sense of wonder at the process of endless creation, and particularly the appreciation that human beings are a part of nature from which they separate themselves at their peril.

This appreciation of nature extends to the realisation that as a part of nature we work with it as opposed to trying to control it from a position of isolation. Ohsawa writes that a healthy attitude is one where anyone can appreciate and remain positive even in the most difficult circumstances.He states that it is these difficulties that help us learn and develop into more experienced people able to take on bigger challenges in life. For example a serious health problem might make someone look for help to improve their health, and as a result lead a much healthier lifestyle so that they eventually end up feeling more healthy than before they became ill. This is exactly what happened to Hugh Faulkner. The idea is to simply try and appreciate the opportunities for positive change in any situation however negative it may seem.

When these seven conditions of health are put together they paint a picture of someone who has an abundance of energy, a good appetite for food and life itself, a short deep uninterrupted sleep each night, a good accurate memory, a naturally positive, happy, cheerful nature, the ability to concentrate, think clearly, and make decisions, and finally live their life with an endless spirit of appreciation so that however difficult life becomes they are always positively using the situation to improve themselves, so that they are grateful for the difficulties.

As a definition of health it certainly sets high standards. No one I know has ever achieved it. However it creates an image of what excellence in health could be. We all achieve a certain level of Ohsawa's idea of health and at the same time it sets up goals to work towards, as well as some kind of measure to see how you are doing. I find reading through these conditions of health and thinking about how they apply to me at the end of the day provides a measure of how my health is changing from day to day and which aspects of my health need the greatest attention.

During his life Ohsawa wrote nearly three hundred books. He started a school to train people to go out and teach macrobiotics and some of these students are still active today. One of these students is Michio Kushi who studied with Ohsawa in Japan and later moved to North America. Michio Kushi has also written many books, validated the macrobiotic diet in terms of modern nutritional theory, and organised macrobiotic educational programmes in the U.S.A.

All this brings us back to the present. What is a macrobiotic diet? Since Dr Ishizuka's initial work on health and diet much has been done to look around the world at those societies that consistently enjoy good health and research what they eat to achieve this. These societies eat grains and vegetables as their primary foods. This is then supplemented with relatively small amounts of beans, fish, dairy food or meat. Both meat and dairy foods are not often eaten as part of a macrobiotic diet as most of us have already eaten far too much of these foods which are high in saturated fats .

A modern macrobiotic diet has become a mixture of several healthy eating traditions and represents the foods eaten by some of the world's most healthy societies. Most of the foods are as close as possible to their fresh natural state and can be described as living foods. Recently to show my son what this means we took whole brown rice , dried aduki beans, and sunflower seeds all straight from the packet placed them on wet paper and put them in a dark cupboard. Within a few days they had sprouted and begun to grow. The same can be said for the vegetables. I often notice how onions will continue to grow in the larder, or how greens will last longer when placed in water like a bunch of flowers. So most of the macrobiotic foods which are whole are still actually growing or have the potential to grow. This living quality is considered an important factor in the ability of a macrobiotic diet to improve health.

Macrobiotics is still based on George Ohsawa's view that the ability to live life to the full is enhanced by good health and that the foundation for good health is what people do to themselves in terms of what they eat, drink and breathe. And then what they do with this in terms of exercise, attitude to life, and lifestyle.

The foods that most of us eat and that would make up a nutritious macrobiotic diet are listed below. These are the foods that Hugh Faulkner has eaten since starting to eat macrobiotically. However it is important to remember that macrobiotics is not a rigid diet restricted to the list of foods below. In one sense anything could be macrobiotic as long as the effects of that food are well understood and that it will improve health and lead to a fuller life. The aim of eating macrobiotically is quite simply to give your body exactly what it needs.

THE MACROBIOTIC DIET

A guide to proportions.

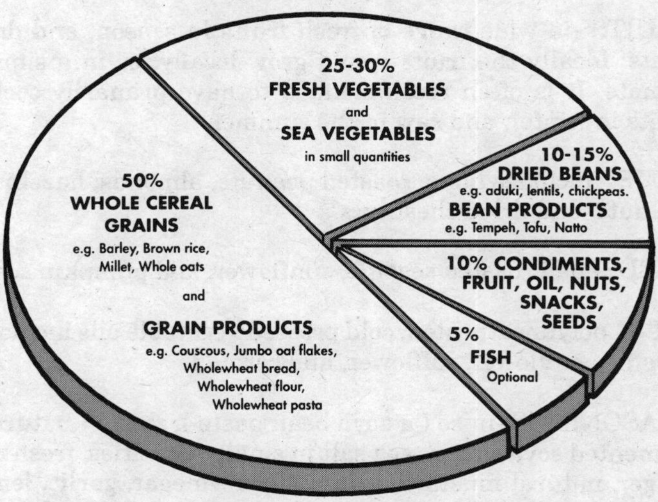

This is an approximate guide showing the proportions of macrobiotic foods recommended on a daily basis by volume. Michio Kushi is acknowledged for creating what he calls the standard macrobiotic diet. This chart is based on his standard diet.

MACROBIOTIC FOODS

BEANS - any dried beans such as aduki, chickpeas, and lentils.

BEVERAGES - natural drinks free from stimulants. Good examples are bancha tea, grain coffee, apple juice, fresh carrot juice, real ales,and spring water.

DESSERTS - a variety of natural desserts made from fruit, juices, wholemeal pastry, and natural sweetners.

GRAINS - primarily whole grains, including barley, brown rice, buckwheat, corn, millet, rye, and whole oats. Other processed grains include oat flakes, whole wheat pasta or noodles, whole wheat flour, couscous, and good quality breads.

FISH - any fresh fish or shellfish.

FRUITS - a wide range of fresh fruits in season, and dried fruits. Ideally the fruits would grow locally, or in a similar climate. It is often recommended to have primarily cooked fruits in winter, and raw in the summer.

NUTS - includes home roasted peanuts, almonds, hazelnuts, walnuts, and dried chestnuts.

SEEDS- pan roasted sesame, sunflower, and pumpkin seeds.

OILS - polyunsaturated, cold pressed vegetable oils including sesame, sunflower, safflower, and corn oil.

SEASONINGS- miso (a soya bean paste), shoyu (naturally fermented soya sauce), sea salt in small quantities, fresh root ginger, natural mustard, tahini, cider vinegar, garlic, lemon juice, brown rice vinegar, and umeboshi vinegar.

SEA VEGETABLES -use wakame in soups, kombu with bean dishes, arame or hiziki with vegetables, dulse in soups or with green vegetables, and agar agar to make an aspic or jelly.

SOYA PRODUCTS - tofu (a soya bean curd), tempeh (a rich fermented bean paste, and natto (fermented beans).

SPREADS - natural sugar free jams, sesame butter, peanut butter and other natural spreads.

SNACKS - rice cakes, roasted seeds and nuts, raisins, sandwiches with natural spreads, and wholemeal bread.

SWEETENERS - barley malt (malt extract), rice syrup, corn and barley syrup, amasake, and fruit juices.

THICKENERS - kuzu and arrowroot.

VEGETABLES - a wide range of fresh vegetables. Ideally grown locally or in a similar climate. Try a mixture of root, ground, and leafy green vegetables.

Chapter 3

HOW DOES MACROBIOTICS WORK?

by Simon Brown

The food on my plate is there as a result of many considerations. Taste, convenience, appearance, smell, and social acceptability all play an important part in deciding what I want to eat, yet the most important reason to eat is to create the kind of health I desire. I need food for physical energy, warmth, and to build and repair each cell.

As far back as The Yellow Emperor's Classic Of Internal Medicine, dated 2600 B.C. Chinese physicians wrote about the importance of food in the role of healing, and preventive medicine. A person's diet was seen as the foundation of good health. In the fifth century B.C. Hippocrates, one of the founding fathers of modern medicine, was responsible for the famous statement "Let food be thy medicine and medicine be thy food". Recently there has been a wealth of research on the link between food and health. Notable institutions like The World Health Organisation (WHO), The U.K. Committee on Medical Aspects of Foods (C.O.M.A.), and the U.S. Senate Select Committee on Nutrition and Human Needs have all confirmed the link between food and health. In addition in 1990 American and Chinese scientists completed the world's largest research project looking at food and health[1]. The results of this are now published by the

1 Brody, Jane. "Huge Study of Diet Indicts Fats and Meat". New York Times, 8 May, 1990

Cornell University Press. This was accomplished with 6500 participants in China and is known as the China project. Again the China project came to the same conclusion.

The food we eat is broken down, and absorbed into the blood. The blood is therefore greatly influenced by what we eat. This blood then nourishes each cell. The quality of the blood will effect the quality of each cell.

For example eating acid forming foods causes the blood to become more acidic and makes demands on our body to use an alkaline mineral, called calcium, from our bones to try and restore the balance of acid and alkaline in the blood.Similarly a diet high in saturated fats increases blood cholesterol.

So not only would someone using macrobiotic principles want the food to look appetising, smell delicious, and be tasty, but most importantly be healthy.

Lets take a journey with your food through your body and see what a macrobiotic diet has to offer:

In this section I have quoted numerous research projects. There are now so many that hardly a week goes by when I do not read about the conclusions of some new research in the daily newspapers. Some of these conclusions are contradictory and when they are all put together can paint a confusing picture. I have primarily used the World Health Organisation (WHO) report on 'Diet, Nutrition, and the Prevention of Chronic Diseases' as a source of research information. In this publication the World Health Organisation has looked at a wide variety of evidence to reach their recommendations. This includes clinical trials, and epidemiological studies. Epidemiological studies are the study of large groups of people. For example the diet and health of one country compared to another, or a group of people such as vegetarians whose diet and health is compared with meat eaters. Some of these studies do not isolate diet from other lifestyle factors like exercise or relaxation however once correlated with other types of study the results merit close attention. In the end I have been convinced most by simply looking around the world and finding those societies that consistently enjoy good health and then see what they have in common.

THE MOUTH

Lets start this journey at the mouth. The absence of refined sugar will help to reduce tooth decay. As the macrobiotic diet has good sources of calcium from greens, sea vegetables, seeds, nuts, beans and tofu, it will also help keep the teeth in good condition. Chewing and mixing your food with your saliva will help break down the complex sugars from starches in the grains, vegetables and beans. After 30-50 chews they actually taste sweet in the mouth.

THE STOMACH

From your mouth your food moves into the stomach. The absence of refined sugar, the small amount of alcohol, coffee and tea all help to reduce the risk of stomach ulcers. It is generally thought that refined sugar is absorbed through the stomach wall and the macrobiotic view is that this increases the likelihood of stomach disorders. In addition, eating meat can cause an over secretion of acids through the stomach lining contributing to ulcers and eventually cancer. In macrobiotics , Japanese umeboshi plums are used to reduce stomach acidity and help minor stomach disorders. These salty pickled plums are particularly good for the over consumption of alcohol, sugar and sweets. It is thought that when under stress people secrete more acid into their stomach and so increasing the risk of stomach disorders.

THE DUODENUM

From the stomach your food passes through the duodenum where it mixes with bile for the digestion of fats and pancreatic juices for the digestion of fats, starches and proteins. As the macrobiotic diet is so low in fats (typically less than 10% of total calories compared to over 40% in a typically British diet) the demands on the liver and gall bladder are greatly reduced. The macrobiotic view is that a more simple diet allows the liver, gallbladder and pancreas to function smoothly without undue stress to meet excessive demands made on them by a diet overly rich in fats, protein and sugar.

THE SMALL INTESTINE

The food now begins its journey through the small intestine where it is absorbed into the blood. The health of the small intestine is influenced by the amount of fibre in the diet. This keeps the lining clean. As the macrobiotic diet consists mainly of grains, beans and vegetables, it is high in fibre.

FIBRE	*g / 100g*
GRAINS	
Brown Rice (Boiled)	1.5
Corn on the Cob (Boiled)	4.7
Oat meal (Porridge)	0.8
Wholemeal Flour	9.6
Wholemeal Bread	8.5
VEGETABLES	
Broccoli Tops (Boiled)	4.1
Brussels Sprouts (Boiled)	2.9
Cabbage (Raw)	3.4
Carrots	3.1
Leek (Boiled)	3.9
Onions	1.3
Parsley (Raw)	9.1

FIBRE	*g / 100g*
BEANS	
Butter beans (Boiled)	5.1
Chickpeas (Boiled)	6.0
Lentils (Boiled)	3.7
Split peas (Boiled)	5.1
FRUIT	
Apples (Raw)	2.0 (Peel 3.7)
Peaches (Steamed)	5.3
Raisins (Dried)	6.8

Meat, chicken, fish, dairy foods, eggs contain none.

The Composition of Foods. Ministry of Agriculture Fisheries and Food, and Medical Research Council. (Published by H.M.S.O.), and U.S. Department of Agriculture.

THE LARGE INTESTINE

The food that is not absorbed into the blood carries on to the large intestine (also known as the colon) where water and salts are absorbed. Again a high fibre diet like the macrobiotic diet will keep the linings clean and healthy. According to World Health Organisation a diet low in fibre containing foods and high in fat increases the risk of colon cancer. The worst kind of fats are saturated fats.

An interesting test you can try on yourself to assess the health of your own large intestine (colon) is to eat uncooked or lightly cooked corn on the cob. Try to swallow the kernels whole. You will then be able to see them in your stools. Make a note of the time taken between eating them and when they next appear after a bowel movement. Ideally this should be 12-24 hours. Anything longer would indicate a sluggish large intestine. It is more likely that toxins accumulate and possibly enter the blood stream when food stays in the colon for a longer period of time. Meat typically takes 48 hours to pass through the large intestine.

Studies in Britain for the Department of Health Committee of Medical Aspects of Food Policy show a direct relationship between dietary fibre and the weight of stools. This weight is significant in avoiding constipation. The World Health Organisation (WHO) recommend a minimum average faecal output of 150g/day. The British study found that a daily intake of 37g of fibre was required to achieve this.

THE LIVER

From the small intestine food that is absorbed into the blood, travels along the portal vein to the liver where the protein, carbohydrates and fats are metabolised (intermediate stage). This organ also stores nutrients and acts on the condition of the blood. The macrobiotic view is that a diet high in spices,stimulants, sugar and alcohol will overstimulate and adversely affect the liver. In addition macrobiotic practitioners feel a diet high in fat not only overworks the liver by forcing it to produce extra bile, but that the fat in the blood actually clogs the liver itself. The WHO notes that gallstones are higher in countries eating greater quantities of saturated fat, and that in these countries vegetarians have a lower incidence of gallbladder stones.

THE HEART

Once in the blood stream the food travels through the circulation system. A diet high in fats causes coronary heart disease, as arteries harden and become clogged straining the heart. It is now thought that a diet with less than 10% of its energy coming from fats, along with appropriate exercise can actually reverse this process.

The World Health Organisation notes that in rural parts of China the incidence of coronary heart disease is only 4% of that observed in Great Britain. In addition the WHO describes how populations with an average saturated fat intake between 3% and 10% of energy intake enjoyed low mortality rates from coronary heart disease. Once their saturated fat intake was greater than 10% of energy intake, a marked increase in coronary heart disease mortality was observed.

In the same publication the World Health Organisation refers to a study showing how British vegetarians have a 30% lower rate of coronary heart disease mortality than non-vegetarians even though an allowance is made for their lower rates of cigarette smoking . Serum cholesterol levels, which are strongly related to the incidence of coronary heart disease , are significantly lower in vegans than in vegetarians, who eat dairy food, or non vegetarians .

Even though some people in Mediterranean countries who have a low incidence of coronary heart disease eat a diet in which a high proportion of their energy comes from fat (more than 40%) the source of this fat is predominantly mono-saturated fatty acids such as olive oil. It would seem that saturated fats which are high in meat and dairy foods are most likely to increase the risk of coronary heart disease.

HIGH BLOOD PRESSURE

High blood pressure is linked to an increased risk of strokes and coronary heart disease. The World Health Organisation concludes its chapter on high blood pressure by recommending a diet low in fat and high in complex carbohydrates, mostly found in grains, beans and vegetables, and to minimise the intake of alcohol. They also suggested a low salt intake.

THE PANCREAS

As the blood moves around the body it is influenced by two hormones excreted from the pancreas, insulin and glucagon. These control blood sugar levels. Sugar comes in three varieties: starch, a complex sugar (polysaccharide); lactose, a more simple sugar (disaccharide); and glucose, a simple sugar (monosaccharide).

Starches are found in grains, beans and vegetables and tend to burn off slowly in the body leading to more stable blood sugar levels and greater physical endurance.Simple sugars are often absorbed through the stomach and tend to raise the blood sugar levels quickly. This strains the pancreas and leads to an increased risk of diabetes mellitus. The macrobiotic diet is very low in simple sugars as it would not normally include refined sugar. However, due to the large amounts of grains, beans and vegetables it is very high in starches or complex sugars, leading to more stable blood sugar levels and greater endurance. All these sugars which are often called complex carbohydrates produce energy for warmth and activity. Their quality greatly affects the kind of energy produced. This is partly why people often notice an increase in energy when starting a macrobiotic diet. Starches are very popular with athletes who need high energy levels over a long period of time. The complex sugars breakdown slowly in the body and can therefore be fully used without taxing the organs that control blood sugar levels. The macrobiotic view is that refined sugars actually weaken the body over a long period of time and also reduce people's ability to concentrate, as refined sugars demineralise the body.

THE BRAIN

The blood that travels through the brain inevitably affects the condition of these cells too. A healthy brain should be able to concentrate well, think clearly and memorise and recall information. Studies with school children showed how their concentration levels increase when nutritional supplements are added to their diet.

Natural whole foods in the macrobiotic diet provide high levels of all nutrients in their natural form. This is important as the digestion system has evolved over 3.2 million years learning to absorb nutrients from real foods as opposed to processed foods with added nutritional supplements or from nutritional supplements in pill form. It is therefore advisable to properly use and exercise the digestive system with real, natural whole foods.

THE LUNGS

As the blood continues its journey around the body it goes back through the heart and is pumped through the lungs where it absorbs oxygen and releases carbon dioxide. The quality of blood greatly affects its ability to absorb oxygen. Fatty blood creates a condition where the haemoglobin sticks together effectively reducing the surface area available to absorb oxygen. In addition a diet high in saturated fats is thought in macrobiotics to be responsible for clogging the lining of the lungs and creating a more sticky condition.

Fatty foods such as meat or dairy foods are often associated with allergies and asthma. In Sweden researchers at the University Hospital in Linkoping found that 90% of the patients whose asthma required cortisone treatment experienced major improvements in the frequency and severity of their asthma attacks when they eliminated meats, eggs and dairy food from their diet.

In addition the Journal of the American Medical Association reported that vegetarians have distinctly lower rates of lung cancer, whether non smokers are compared with non smoking meat eaters or vegetarians who smoke are compared with meat eaters who smoke. According to research by J. Strawler elevated cholesterol may increase the risk of lung cancer in smokers. The World Health Organisation also conclude that dietary fats and dietary cholesterol have been associated with lung cancer risk.

THE BREAST

Recently the incidence of breast cancer has been linked to a high fat diet. The studies by Dr Takeshi Hirayoma at the National Cancer Research Institute in Tokyo found that women eating meat daily were four times more likely to suffer from breast cancer than those women who ate little or no meat. Similar results were found for the consumption of eggs, butter and cheese. In addition a report in the British Medical Journal, ('Changing Age of the Menopause') it was found that women whose diets are high in fat and protein reach menopause at an average age of 50 whereas those eating little or no animal fats begin menopause at an average age of 46. Unfortunately the later menopause begins the more likely the person is to suffer from breast cancer.

The WHO reports that there is evidence of a direct association between breast cancer mortality and the intake of energy, fats and specific sources of dietary fats such as milk and beef. For example, in the U.K. during 1978, 28 women per 100,000 died from breast cancer. The average consumption of fats was 40% of the total energy. Conversely Yugoslavia where only 27% of their energy intake is fat has a death rate of less than half that of the U.K. (11 per 100,000 women). Japan where 24% of their energy intake comes from fat, has a death rate of only 6 per 100,000 women.

THE BONES

Your blood provides the mineral calcium for your bones. A lack of calcium in the bones leads to a condition called osteoporosis where the bones become brittle and weak as they lose their density. Unfortunately, already 25% of American women have lost more than 50% of their bone density.

Researchers examining the relationship between the diet and the health of 6500 Chinese people found that osteoporosis was uncommon even though the Chinese ate only half the calcium typical in an American diet. Interestingly five separate studies reported in the Journal of Nutrition show that a person's calcium balance increased by an average of 19 mg with an intake of 920 mg of calcium whilst eating a low protein diet whereas when eating a diet with the same 920 mg of calcium, but a high protein diet, they actually lost 94 mg of calcium. The World Health Organisation also reports that high protein and high-salt diet are known to increase bone loss. The logical conclusion being that if your calcium comes from high protein sources like milk, cheese and yogurt you might even lose more than you take in. This partly explains why osteoporosis is so common in those countries with a high consumption of diary foods. There are many excellent low protein sources of calcium. Most common are leafy green vegetables, beans, nuts and seeds.

THE SKIN

The skin is one way your blood can eliminate water, oils and possibly toxins. Typically the body eliminates 833 g of fluid each day through the skin. A diet high in fats can eventually overwhelm and block this process, denying the body of an important avenue for eliminating unwanted materials. The end result is often dry skin and an inability to sweat from all over the body. One of the most common changes people and their friends notice when starting a macrobiotic diet is the improvement in their skin quality. It may be that a diet so low in fats allows the pores to unclog and breath again. Apart from eating well the quality of the skin can be improved by scrubbing with a hot damp cotton hand towel or flannel from head to toe each day until it is red all over. You will notice that areas of poor circulation take longer to change colour.

THE KIDNEYS

Together with the lungs and skin the kidneys are the main organs for purifying the blood of waste and toxic substances. They also act to maintain a balance of blood acidity. Inevitably any diet that is high in toxic substances, creates an over acidic blood condition will cause the kidneys to do more work.

The British Journal of Urology in 1979 reported that kidney stones occur far less frequently in vegetarians than meat eaters. It may be that as a high protein diet causes the elimination of calcium, this calcium contributes to the formation of kidney stones, when the kidneys remove this from the blood to be eliminated in the urine.

Macrobiotic practitioners advocate the principle of only drinking when thirsty. It is common for people to drink too many fluids. This dilutes the digestive juices, dilutes the blood, places an additional load on the heart and most importantly overworks the kidneys. Lower backaches are common and in my experience these often lessen when liquid consumption is reduced. It is also common for people to have to get up in the night and interrupt their deep sleep to urinate. Again this is an obvious sign of excessive liquid consumption.

THE JOINTS

Your blood is instrumental in keeping joints healthy. In 1981 the British Medical Journal noted the link between diet and rheumatoid arthritis. This suggested that diary foods actually aggravate arthritis. Studies in China have shown that the incidence of rheumatoid arthritis is low where a diet low in animal food is consumed.

The macrobiotic view is that high fat foods like meat, diary food and eggs tend to reduce blood circulation to the joints, Whereas foods like sugar, alcohol, coffee, citrus fruits and juices would swell or weaken the joints.

WEIGHT

Excess weight is commonly associated with coronary heart disease, high blood pressure, diabetes mellitus and in extremes with gallstones, cancer of the breast, uterus, prostrate, gallbladder and kidneys. The World Health Organisation recommends a measure of body weight called body-mass index (B.M.I). This is your weight in kg divided by the square of your height in metres.

$$\text{B.M.I.} = \frac{\text{Body mass in kg}}{\text{Height in metres squared}}$$

For example I weigh 70kg and I am 1.82m high. I therefore have a B.M.I. of 21.

The WHO recommends a B.M.I of between 20-25. One interesting revelation from the China project is that Chinese people consume 20% more calories than Americans but Americans are 25% fatter even when the weights are adjusted for their different heights. It was noticed that the main differences were the consumption of fat and starch (Starch is another term for complex carbohydrates which are mostly found in grains, beans and vegetables). The Chinese consume only 1/3 of the fat Americans do, whilst eating twice as much starch. The conclusion was that fat, particularly from animal sources, could be the prime influence on excess weight. The World Health Organisation also includes refined sugar as being another major influence.

Again a macrobiotic diet would meet all the requirements for maintaining an appropriate weight. It is low in fats, particularly saturated fat, low in refined carbohydrates (refined sugar) but high in complex carbohydrates from grains, beans and vegetables. Macrobiotics is not necessarily a diet for rapid weight loss, it could be a year or more before someone feels happy with their weight, however it would seem that with this healthy approach the weight stabilises without subsequent increases often experienced with rapid weight loss regimes.

Obviously exercise plays an enormous part in maintaining any kind of weight control. It is important to design an exercise programme that not only burns off body fat but also keeps the body stretched, flexible and supple.

Having been considered as recently as 1980 in Britain to be a rather obscure, strange diet, macrobiotics would now appear to many people as a natural sensible way of eating. It not only reflects many of the recent recommendations by the WHO and COMA but goes further.

Although as Hugh Faulkner points out very little research has been commissioned by macrobiotic organisations there has been a wealth of grass roots practical trial and error. Macrobiotic counsellors and teachers eat what they recommend and continually refine and develop the macrobiotic dietary recommendations.

Chapter 4

RECOVERY

by Hugh Faulkner

Cancer of the pancreas is usually a rapid killer. It is an insidious tumour that frequently causes no pain or other symptoms, at least in the early stages. Hence it is usually diagnosed late, and few people can expect to survive much more than six months after diagnosis. Even fewer survive one year and very few two years. It is now over five years since my diagnosis and I feel very fit, work hard, do some gardening, swimming and go to keep fit classes. I have more energy than I have had for years. The term spontaneous regression is used by doctors when a tumour appears to be quiescent and they don't know why. Spontaneous regression is extremely rare in pancreatic cancer.

SOME OF THE MEDICAL ASPECTS OF THE DIET

I have followed the macrobiotic diet and way of life recommended by Michio Kushi reasonably faithfully - strictly in the first year, and with a few relaxations thereafter. Some, but not all of these relaxations were with Michio's permission. However if I have any minor digestive upsets I treat them as a warning and find that a return to a stricter observation of the diet soon puts me right. Michio's book, "The Cancer Prevention Diet" deals more fully with it. This can be modified by an experienced counsellor to suit the patient's particular needs. Apart from a few details, the macrobiotic diet closely follows modern progressive dietetic advice. Your own family doctor or your cancer surgeon will not necessarily be familiar with macrobiotics or even with orthodox modern dietetics. John Robbins in his book "A Diet for a New America" says that in 1981 only 30 of the 125 medical schools in the United States had a single required course in nutrition, and that a recent Senate investigation revealed that the average doctor in the States received less than three hours training in nutrition during four years of medical school. This situation is very similar in the medical schools in Europe. We heard John lecture at the macrobiotic Summer Conference at Amherst, Boston, in August 1990 and I have drawn heavily on his excellent and well documented book.

The situation is little if any better in the medical schools of Italy and Britain, the two countries I know best. All of us, including doctors, are exposed to the same propaganda extolling the virtues of meat and dairy products. Indeed the Milk Marketing Board in Britain makes a special attempt to convince doctors. Some fifteen years ago as an editor of a medical journal I was offered a free holiday (which I refused) at one of their health establishments. The Meat Marketing Board in the States buys full page colour advertisements in J.A.M.A. (The Journal of the American Medical Association) widely read by doctors.

Looking back it is almost incredible that it has taken us so long to realise the implications of information readily available in professional journals several years ago. In the First World War the allied blockade of Denmark cut off all imports, and the Government diverted all available grain to people instead of cattle. During the period of severest rationing - October 1917 to October 1918 - the overall mortality rate was the lowest ever recorded.[1] During the German occupation of Norway in the Second World War, meat was almost unobtainable. Once again the death rate

1 Hindhede, Mikkel. *The Effect of Food Restrictions during War on Mortality in Copenhagen.*

from circulatory disease dropped dramatically. After the war, when Norwegians returned to their normal meat diet, their death rate rose accordingly.[2] Studies of populations living mainly on a vegetarian diet in Ecuador, the USSR and North Pakistan have revealed that they live longer and remain active in their eighties and nineties. Yet the popular image of long- haired sandalled vegetarian weaklings dies hard. John Robbins lists over twenty world class athletes who were vegetarians. Yet our neighbours in Chianti still firmly believe that their menfolk need meat protein and animal fats to do a day's work on the land. This belief has no scientific basis, and I have seen no studies in the medical journals to support it.

During the small amount of teaching on nutrition I received in my own medical school, I was taught that animal proteins were first-class, and vegetable proteins second-class and therefore presumably inferior. This distinction, apparently based on experiments with rats, now appears to have been almost completely abandoned. Leading nutritionists state today that it is almost impossible to design a diet which provides adequate calories but which is deficient in protein. (John Robbins *"Diet for a New America"*) It seems impossible to claim that one source of protein is superior to another, or that vegetarians have difficulty in obtaining protein. Obviously in the third world and amongst the very poor in our own societies, people are simply not getting enough food - and therefore not enough protein.

Another worry some people have about a macrobiotic diet is the possibility of calcium deficiency. We have been brought up to believe that cows' milk is an essential source of calcium, which prevents osteoporosis - particularly in older women. In fact, the main cause of osteoporosis has been found to be excessive protein![3]

2 Strom, A. and Jensen, R.A. *Mortality From Circulatory Diseases in Norway.*

3 Johnson, N. et al. *Effect of Level of Protein Intake on Urinary and Fecal Calcium Retention.*

John Robbins quotes four other studies which show that even with high calcium intake, increased protein intake results in osteoporosis. High protein diets in general - and meat based diets in particular - lead to decrease in bone density and osteoporosis.[4]

There is also evidence that excess protein can lead to certain cancers. According to Professor Campbell of Cornell University: "there is a strong correlation between dietary protein intake and cancer of the breast, prostate, pancreas and colon."[5] Indeed Michio Kushi believes my pancreatic cancer was caused by eating too many eggs and too much chicken.

Nutrition, like immunology, genetics and molecular biology, is a relatively new scientific discipline. As we have already said, it is comparatively neglected in most medical schools and few doctors are equipped to deal with it in practice. However it is generally known that good wholesome food can support the immune system, and it is perhaps less well known that food heavily processed, contaminated with pesticides, high in animal protein and fat, cholesterol and refined sugars can depress it. In recent years a number of books and articles in scientific journals have begun to describe the relationship between diet and immunity, but we are only at the beginning, and far more research is needed.

In the sixties we first became conscious of the link between animal fats and heart disease. Saturated fat and cholesterol raise the blood cholesterol, favouring the formation of arteriosclerosis, leading to a narrowing and blocking of arteries. When this occurs in the heart, the result is "coronary thrombosis", popularly known as "a heart attack". In the brain this gives rise to strokes. The three conditions - heart attacks, stroke and cancer - are the principle causes of death in the industrially developed countries. (R. Walford - "Maximum Life Span" - see book-list) From 1963 to 1965

4 Altschuler, S. *Dietry Protein and Calcium Loss: a Review.*
5 Lang, S. *Diet and Disease.*

the International Arteriosclerosis Project examined the arteries of over 20,000 autopsied bodies throughout the world. The results clearly showed a correlation between diets high in saturated fat and cholesterol and arteriosclerosis, heart attacks and strokes. (P. Hausman - "Jack Sprat's Legacy - the Science and Politics of Fat and Cholesterol" - see book-list). This and other studies caused consternation in the ranks of meat and dairy producers, who hastened to point out that coconuts, palm kernels and chocolate also contain cholesterol. This only served to draw attention to the fact that these are the only plant foods significantly high in cholesterol.

During the past twenty years a whole number of studies have demonstrated that arteriosclerosis results from a dietary intake of saturated fat and cholesterol. The dairy, meat and poultry industries in industrialised countries have vigorously contested this, and financed several studies attempting to disprove it - but without success. They have demonstrated that carnivorous animals do not get arteriosclerosis however much meat they eat - but failed to show that human beings are among them. Of all the factors known to be involved in heart disease - obesity, lack of exercise, refined sugar, coffee, smoking, raised blood pressure, lack of dietary fibre - saturated fat and cholesterol are far the most important.

Although the main outlines are clear, research is still proceeding in this area, and there are conflicting opinions on the details of the processes involved. I am certainly not equipped to deal with the technicalities in this field and anyone specially interested in this important subject should consult one of the recent books published. For our immediate purpose it is enough to know that there are basically two kinds of dietary fat: saturated and unsaturated. Most of the fat in red meat, lard, butter, cow's milk, hard cheeses and poultry is saturated. These are invariably accompanied by cholesterol. On the other hand, the fats in grains, vegetables and fruit are unsaturated - with the exception of palm and coconut oil these fats are easier to assimilate. Polyunsaturated fat is the least dense form of unsaturated fat and hence the easiest to assimilate. A molecule is said to be "saturated" when all its available carbon bonds are occupied by hydrogen atoms; unsaturated fats have more carbon bonds left free. (Michio Kushi and Martha Cottrell - *"Aids, Macrobiotics and Natural Immunity"* - see book-list).

Macrobiotic counsellors recommend that almost all vegetables and fruits should be lightly cooked. Ideally they should be home grown, or obtained from a reliable organic grower. All locally grown fruit and vegetables are acceptable with the exception of the nightshade or solanaceous family, which includes potatoes, tomatoes, peppers, aubergine, courgettes - introduced to Europe comparatively recently. All tropical plants, fruits, palm and coconut oils are also excluded.

John Robbins has carefully collected a mass of evidence to support his case, despite the fact that his family is said to own the largest multinational company manufacturing ice-cream in the world! I have only selected a small part of this evidence, attempting to show that the macrobiotic diet, though originally based on Japanese traditional medicine, is entirely consistent with these relatively recent discoveries in the field of nutrition. It can no longer be dismissed as quaint Eastern folklore without relevance for us today.

THE BIOLOGY OF HOPE

While I am convinced that the macrobiotic diet has played an important role in my case, I believe that many other factors have also had a share in my recovery. These I have grouped under Norman Cousins' title, "The Biology of Hope."[6] Norman Cousins was for many years the Editor of the Saturday Review, and in another book - "Anatomy of an Illness" - describes how he cured himself of a serious collagen illness - a disease of the connective tissue. In 1970 he resigned from his editorship, and although he had no

6 Cousins, Norman. *Head First - The Biology of Hope.*

medical qualification, was invited to join the faculty of the Department of Psychiatry and Biobehavioural Science of UCLA (the University of California, Los Angeles.) Here he had the opportunity of playing an active part in the teaching and research of the department, and in particular the growing field of psychoneuroimmunology. For some time a number of researchers outside mainstream immunology have been observing the influence of various psychological processes on immune responses. Gradually psychologists, neurophysiologists and immunologists have begun to see the fundamental links between their various fields. Out of this realization the relatively new science of psychoneuro-immunology (PNI) has emerged.[7]

At the 7th International Congress of Immunology in Berlin in August, 1989 there were over 160 papers dealing with interactions between the immune and the nervous systems. Psychoneuroimmunology "represents a much more differentiated, more finely tuned articulation of disease and healing processes, increasingly dissolving the three long-standing dualisms of mind and body, body and environment, individual and population. For the first time, medicine is equipped with a discourse capable of formulating very specific correlations between (i) the patient's bodily experienced meanings and (ii) conditions or states of the medical body, the body that figures in the research and clinical practices of medicine."[8]

We have long realised that anxiety, depression and stress can have a direct effect on our physiology. Hans Selye made a great contribution in this field and many years ago I heard him lecture - fortunately in English - in his old university in Prague. Faced with a patient who has a terminal illness - at least in the terms of western medicine - a doctor has a difficult choice. Should he tell the patient the truth as he sees it? Or should he compromise, and leave him a modicum of hope -

7 Booth, Roger. *Psychoneuroimmunology.*
8 Levin, D.M. and Solomon, G.F. Esalen Institute. (non-dated paper)

however small? American doctors say that their lawyers advise them to tell the truth, the whole truth and nothing but the truth, to protect themselves from possible lawsuits from patients' families. Yet in doing so they may be lowering their patient's resistance and making recovery less likely. No doctor can possibly give a precise estimate of survival time, and many of us have always tried to avoid anything in the nature of a death sentence, without departing too far from the facts as we see them.

In fact my own doctors at the Whittington Hospital never told me my illness was terminal in so many words. Maybe this was because they knew I would look up the prognosis in the medical literature - and anyway I never asked. When I learned that I could expect to live two to six months from the date of diagnosis, this only confirmed what I already knew, so I was not particularly shocked. However at this stage, it never occurred to me that I could do anything to change this, and I accepted the verdict of orthodox medicine without question.

When I first read that some people believed that macrobiotics could help the body to reject cancer, it was a revelation. I certainly wasn't intellectually convinced, but perhaps here there was something I could do, here was hope, however slim - and anyway what did I have to lose? Looking back, the first result of our decision to try macrobiotics - and my family and friends fully supported this - was the feeling that I had regained control of the situation, even if at this stage this could have been completely illusory. But I was doing something, whether leading to success or failure I didn't know.

In my interview with Ed Esko - my first meeting with a macrobiotic counsellor - I was conscious of something else. Ed's complete certainty that I would recover came across to us both - and from that moment we both had real hope for the first time since my diagnosis. Hence I believe that Ed Esko began my recovery, and told him so when we met again at the Macrobiotic Summer Conference at Amherst last year.

I can't prove scientifically that the renewal of hope had a direct effect on my immune system. Although the science of PNI is only in its infancy it could provide some exciting scientific findings in the next few years. A number of studies carried out by the psychoneuroimmunology unit in the University of California have clearly demonstrated the effect of positive emotions on the immune system.[9] On the other hand emotional distress resulted in negative immune functions. This latter finding was more evident in older people, in whom the relationship between psychological factors and immune functions seems stronger than in younger people. However, the immune systems of older people in good health are as functional, and in some ways actually superior, to those of healthy persons half their age. The immune systems of both old and young were comparably enhanced following a bout of vigorous physical exercise.

This work has confirmed my own belief that in my case, hope, albeit combined with a macrobiotic diet and life-style, played a vital role in my recovery. When I see patients who have been told that they have terminal cancer, I naturally tell them of this work and my own experience, but I am careful to remind them that we are all different, and there is no guarantee that their results will be the same - but there is always, or nearly always, hope!

LIFE-STYLE

Macrobiotic counsellors always stress that macrobiotics does not consist only of the diet. The English word 'diet' derives from the medieval Latin 'diaetare' which, according to the Oxford English Dictionary, meant "to live according to a certain plan" and was not limited to food consumption. Since traditional Eastern medicine regards all illness as a break in the harmony of the relationship between the individual and nature as a whole, it seeks to help the body to restore that harmony. This should be easier for us living in a calm peaceful corner of the Chianti hills, surrounded by

9 Cousins, Norman. Ibid.

woods and birds and wild animals - when the hunters leave us in peace. We have consciously tried to draw closer to the wild life, and have built artificial nests for the birds and bats, and homes for the hedgehogs. We walk in the woods, though with all our other activities, not often enough.

I have taken more regular exercise since my illness. I was never a keen swimmer, but in my old age I have found great satisfaction in swimming. I miss it when we can't find time for it or when we are travelling. In the first year we tried to follow Michio's injunction to reduce travelling to a minimum, but I pointed out that a major part of our travelling then consisted in trying to meet up with him in various parts of Europe for consultations!

Macrobiotic counsellors usually strongly recommend the use of natural fabrics. Clothing made from artificial fibres is believed to reduce the flow of energy between the skin and the natural environment, while natural fibres like cotton, linen, silk and wool allow the energy to flow freely. We try to follow this advice as far as possible. We also try to avoid chemically produced cosmetics, soaps and shampoos. Natural vegetable products are now widely available.

Lastly, and by no means least, since my illness I have drawn closer to family and friends. This is not necessarily the result of macrobiotics, but its general philosophy has helped. My relationship with Marian has deepened and strengthened, and she has willingly and cheerfully taken part in every aspect of our new life - including valiantly attempting to master the mysteries of our new word processor and all the trials and tribulations of producing a book. Without her love and active support it would have all been very much more difficult.

Chapter 5

A GENERAL LOOK AT MACROBIOTICS

by Hugh Faulkner

Since I believe that macrobiotics and the macrobiotic way of life has played an important role in my apparent recovery from pancreatic cancer, it seems reasonable to try to find out how this has come about. Modern macrobiotics is based on traditional Japanese medicine and this seems the logical starting point of my enquiry. Japanese and Chinese medicine have a great deal in common and I have found Ted Kaptchuk's book invaluable as an introduction to Eastern traditional medicine as a whole.[1]

Apart from the bare essentials of elementary acupuncture technique, the theoretical depth and clinical potential of a complex medical system are almost completely unknown to doctors in the West. For the most part traditional Eastern medicine is seen as a quaint survival of folklore and magic. Modern Western scientific medicine provides the only source of truth in the field of health. A growing number of people in the West question this view, partly because Western medicine, despite its very real achievements, has failed to prevent or cure the chronic degenerative conditions which cause most deaths and disability in our societies. A minority has turned to the East, seeing Eastern philosophy and medicine as more mysterious, more spiritual, more holistic

1 Kaptchuk, T. *The Web that has no Weaver.*

and therefore more "true" than western medicine. This approach seems to me to be mistaken and tends to turn a rational discipline - albeit based on premises vastly different from our own - into a religious faith. Dr. Kaptchuk sees Chinese medicine - and I believe this can be equally applied to Japanese medicine - as "a coherent and independent system of thought and practice that has been developed over two millenia. It is however based on the philosophy, theory and practice of civilisations completely different from our own. The main difference in perception and labelling between traditional Chinese medicine and Western biomedicine is the understanding of the relation/identity of psyche and soma."[2]

I have only been actively looking for information about life-style and cancer since my own diagnosis five years ago. I now realise that many alternative approaches to cancer had appeared before this, and that there has been a considerable amount of research into the effect of the mind on physiological processes. But little of this had been known to the general public or to doctors, who, if they knew about it at all, regarded it as unproven folk-lore, and of little interest.

In February 1990 an international conference was organised in London by the British Journal of Hospital Medicine - generally regarded as a conservative journal - on the subject of "Cancer and the Mind". Cancer specialists, psychiatrists, psychologists, immunologists, sociologists, complementary practitioners and patients attended - in all over 500 doctors and nurses. This shows the enormous interest in this subject in the orthodox medical profession, and makes the need for extending the dialogue between complementary medicine and orthodox Western medicine increasingly necessary. Not all the speakers agreed with one another, but a majority consensus appeared to have accepted the fact that behaviour and

2 Ots, Thomas. *The Angry Liver, the Anxious Heart and the Melancholy Spleen.*

attitude could possibly affect the onset or progress of cancer. Diet was not dealt with at the conference but several speakers made observations highly relevant to our work in macrobiotics.

A cancer patient, Dr. Dennison, quoted Carl Rogers' definition of a good therapist. He defines three essential qualities of a person centred approach. First, 'genuineness' - no professional front or personal facade. Second, 'acceptance' - unconditional positive regard towards the patient. Third, 'empathetic understanding'. He says, "This kind of sensitive, active listening is extremely rare in our lives. We think we listen, but very rarely do we listen with real understanding, true empathy. Yet listening of this very special kind is one of the most potent forces for change that I know." Many doctors would find this kind of listening extremely difficult, and perhaps our failure to listen to our patients is one of the reasons why so many people are turning to complementary medicine. I hope macrobiotic counsellors find it easier to listen in this way, and it should certainly have an important place in their training.

Patrick Pietroni, the founder of the Holistic Medical Association in Britain, made an interesting point on the shift from what he called 'masculine' interventions - chemotherapy, radiotherapy and surgery, to the 'feminine' therapies - listening, caring, holding, touching, massaging and imagery. This strengthened my belief that more women should become macrobiotic counsellors, and not see their only place as in the kitchen. Dr. Pietroni further suggested that all of us working in this area should ask ourselves three questions:

1. Do our interventions affect the lives of cancer patients?
2. Do these interventions affect their long-term survival?
3. Does the long-term practice of these techniques prevent the occurrence of cancer?

In macrobiotics fully accurate answers to these questions are not yet available. Clearly there are far more factors involved than in most medical clinical trials and research is far more complicated. Nevertheless we have to go on trying to answer these questions. Until we do my medical colleagues will not take us entirely seriously.

Several speakers believed that some form of group psychotherapy can facilitate and reinforce the development of a 'fighting spirit' and defeat the feeling of 'helplessness' experienced by cancer patients. I know some macrobiotic counsellors are interested in humanistic psychotherapy and are already using some of the techniques involved. It would be interesting to look at the possibility of offering cancer patients participation in a support group in addition to normal advice on diet and life-style. This would probably only be possible in a centre with many cancer patients, and might require the help of a psychologist trained in group therapy. If behaviour therapy can change people's attitudes and life-styles, such groups could also have a preventive role.

Dr. Moorey, a lecturer in psychological medicine at the Royal Marsden Hospital, quoted Albert Schweitzer when he said that the greatest discovery of any generation is that human beings can change their lives by altering their attitudes of mind. The medicine I was taught in a London medical school fifty years ago was concerned mainly with defining disease categories, disclosing their pathology, and determining wherever possible a precise cause and cure for a specific disease. The mind was barely mentioned. I created a sensation by asking to learn about psychiatry, which proved to be quite impossible in the London Hospital Medical College in those days. Our teaching was firmly based on the newtonian cartesian mechanistic approach. Eastern medicine is concerned with the physiology and psychology of each individual patient. All available information from the history and a detailed examination is used to reveal what is called a "pattern of disharmony". This approach is essentially "holistic" and no single finding can be interpreted without relating it to the whole. It is based on the Taoist concept of Yin and Yang.

As I see it, Yin and Yang are neither physical forces nor material entities. They are simply convenient labels to explain the continuous movement of constant change, in Marxist terminology the interpenetration of opposites, and the relationship of all things to one another and the whole.[3]

Yin is the name given to energy or movement that is expanding. Yang is the name given to energy or movement that is contracting. Yin is associated with cold, rest, passivity, darkness, plants, female. Yang with heat, stimulation, activity, light and animals. All things have a Yin aspect and Yang aspect, including illnesses.

Ki, the life force, is said to flow through the meridians and forms the basis of all acupuncture and shiatsu treatment. As far as I know it has not yet been possible to detect or measure Ki or define the meridians scientifically, though the anaesthetic and analgesic actions of acupuncture have been demonstrated. Research workers in Romania, Britain and the United States however claim to have demonstrated the presence of "magnetic fields which can act therapeutically by facilitating the communication between aberrant cells and adjacent normal cells, which can therefore bring about a return to normality."[4]

Macrobiotics has adopted the philosophy and general approach of traditional Eastern medicine, but not all of its applications in practice. Ron Kotzsch, in his excellent book, describes in some detail how macrobiotics has evolved over the years.[5] Any reader who wants more information on the history of macrobiotics and in particular of the fascinating - and sometimes surprising - lives of the founding fathers is strongly recommended to read Ron Kotzsch's book.

The general Japanese diet in the mid 19th century appears to have closely resembled a macrobiotic diet. Cattle were bred for work, not for meat, and dairy products were unknown. When in 1859 the American ambassador asked for

3 Levins, R. and Lewontin, R. *The Dialectical Biologist.*
4 Oldfield and Coghill. *The Dark Side of the Brain.*
5 Kotzsch, R. *Macrobiotics - Yesterday and Today.*

a cow to provide milk for his tea the Japanese diplomats were incredulous. Despite this the Japanese rapidly adopted Western ways. In 1871 the first German physicians arrived to teach and to practice Western medicine and surgery. By 1883 traditional medicine was banned, and only Western medicine permitted.

Although George Ohsawa is generally regarded as the founder of macrobiotics, Kotzsch has chosen Ekken Kaibara (1630-1716) as its earliest forerunner. He travelled widely and wrote books on botany, geography, herbal remedies and morals. At the age of 83 he wrote a book which was translated into English with the title "Japanese Secrets of Good Health." In Chapter One he says "..it is only natural that one who has learned health preservation and who applies it, will become strong in body, will shirk off all diseases, will live to the age Providence meant him to live to, and enjoy it too..! Sickness like health is something that mankind creates. Quoting the Tao Te Ching, Kaibara notes that "One's life is in one's own hands". Perhaps the only part of his advice unacceptable to us today lies in his strict rules for sexual intercourse. According to Kotzsch "If all the restrictions are observed one may indulge only on cloudless overcast evenings during the new moon in a thatched cave opening to the northwest." As far as I know this recommendation is not followed by any of our macrobiotic friends today.

If we accept Kaibara as the grandfather of macrobiotics it seems reasonable to call Doctor Sagen Ishizuka the founder of the modern discipline. Born in 1860, in a period of rapid expansion and modernisation, he felt that much of great value in traditional medicine was being lost. He set out to revive it and present it in a modern scientific form. It was on this foundation that Ohsawa and others built.

Ishizuka studied both traditional and Western medicine and qualified as a doctor. At the age of twenty-eight he became a physician in the Japanese army. He developed a chronic renal condition which Western medicine failed to cure. He began to experiment with his diet and abandoned meat and dairy products and ate mainly brown rice, and recovered. At one time he lived for a month on only sweet potatoes. He also embarked on anthropological and chemical studies and read the Western scientific journals. He published his magnum opus - "A Chemical Nutritional Theory of Long Life" in 1897, at the age of 37. He cites countless experiments of his own and others to support his theories, determined to provide a "respectable" scientific explanation for them. In the following year he produced a practical handbook on diet for the general public, which went through 23 editions. His fame grew in leaps and bounds and he had to limit the number of patients he saw to 100 a day! Letters addressed to "Dr. Miso Soup, Tokyo" reached him. In 1908 a group of his supporters formed the "Food Cure Society," in effect the first macrobiotic organisation.

Several years after the founding of this society, a young student, Yukikazu Sakurazawa, came across a book by Ishizuka. The young man was later known in the West as George Ohsawa. He was born in Kyoto in 1893. From about 1923 until his death in 1966 the history of macrobiotics is virtually the story of Ohsawa's life and works. Both his mother and brother died from pulmonary tuberculosis and he himself contracted the disease. Given little hope by Western medicine he followed Ishizuka's teaching and recovered. Until the age of 30 he was a successful businessman and travelled widely in the West. In 1923 the Tokyo fire and earthquake destroyed the headquarters of his firm and he lost his job. He turned to the Shoku-Yo movement, where he seems to have rapidly become a leading figure. He took over publications and wrote and spoke widely, drawing chiefly from Ishizuka. His political views however changed with bewildering rapidity. At different times he was supporting fascism, anti-semitism, the peace movement, world government and Japanese militarism.

His lack of formal education and any background of general culture is revealed in his writing and teaching. In his book, Zen Macrobiotics, he made the unwise claim that "any disease, even an incurable one, can be cured in 10 days", a claim which no macrobiotic counsellor would dream of making today. Yet at other times he seemed anxious that his work should be accepted by Western scientists. In his teaching and his consultations with patients he could be brutally offensive. Apparently he believed that students and patients could be shocked into positive action. Kotzsch points out that "for some the approach worked, for others not." It is interesting to meet this technique in the psychotherapeutic methods developed by Frank Farrelly in the United States known as "Provocative Therapy".

Why then did Ohsawa have so many devoted students? He seems to have convinced them that he deeply cared - for them and for his patients. They referred to him as "Papa". Although he dreamed of making macrobiotics a mass movement, apparently his charisma and his numerous talents did not include any capacity for organisation and administration. The portrait of Ohsawa which emerges is a strangely contradictory one. In Kotzch's summing-up: "He was both maudlin and heartless, loving and cruel, disciplined and self-indulgent, brilliantly insightful and intellectually sloppy." Michio Kushi recalls that "He had so many personalities, so many faces. One moment he looked and acted like a gangster, the next like a saint." All in all, most people in macrobiotics seem to see Ohsawa's contribution as positive, though many today would reject his belief in the virtues of cigarette smoking and salt - to say nothing of his flirtations with fascism and Japanese militarism. He died suddenly after returning home from lecturing at the age of 73, probably from coronary thrombosis, though no post mortem was carried out. It seems likely that his cigarette smoking contributed to his death.

Although Ohsawa never realised his dream of a worldwide macrobiotic revolution, he inspired many young men and women by his lectures and seminars. Aveline Kushi still speaks of him with affection and admiration and is, I believe, planning a celebration in 1993 to mark the centenary of his birth. Some of his students went on to carry the torch of the revival of traditional Japanese medicine. Of these the first and most important was Michio Kushi, to be followed later by Aveline.

Michio Kushi came to the United States in 1949, at the age of 23. He first intended to study international law and world peace. Tomoko Yokoyama, later to be known as Aveline Kushi, was studying with George Ohsawa in Japan at the time, and she first became aware of Michio Kushi due to the interesting letters the young man was sending to her teacher. She was so impressed with these letters that she decided to join Michio in the States, and she made the journey in 1951. Shortly after, another of Ohsawa's students, Herman Aihara, also arrived in the States.

A company started by Kushi and Aihara to import Japanese goods was not a success. Later other ventures, including a small macrobiotic restaurant, were more successful. In 1965 a young woman in New York who was said to be following a macrobiotic diet, died suddenly. Ohsawa was sued for malpractice but was exonerated. However the Federal Food and Drug Administration raided the Ohsawa Foundation and claimed that books and food were being sold as a cure for illness. The Foundation was charged with "false advertising" and closed down. Following this, and Ohsawa's sudden death in 1966, macrobiotic activity in New York virtually ceased, to be revived only several years later by Shizuko Yamamoto.

Meanwhile the Kushis had moved to Boston, which became the main focus of macrobiotics on the East coast, while Aihara developed increasing activity in the West. The story of their struggles is told vividly by Ron Kotzch in his book. At this time the Kushis emerged clearly as the leaders of the movement. Michio developed his own individual approach and steadily liberalized the Ohsawa diet. He wrote, lectured and taught continuously, and gradually trained and inspired a whole number of men and women, many of whom have made their own contributions and developed centres in Europe and in other parts of the States. Aveline, as well as being involved in organisation, became the leading exponent of macrobiotic cookery and has written several excellent books on the subject. She told us once in one of her cookery classes, that the last thing she intended to do when she was young was to spend her life in the kitchen! Marian and I were entertained in the Kushi house in Brookline, Boston, during our recent visit to the States. The Kushi Institute has moved from Boston to the new centre at Becket.

Now, some 30 years after Ohsawa first presented macrobiotics in his lectures in New York, considerable progress has been made. There are two major educational centres (Vega and the Kushi Institute), which some 300 students attend every year. The worldwide macrobiotic directory of 1984/5 listed some 175 "macrobiotic centres, friends and businesses" in Canada and the United States, 150 certified teachers and counsellors, and three macrobiotic journals. The annual summer conference in Amherst attracts about 600 people.

In Europe the small beginnings, stimulated by Ohsawa, virtually came to a standstill after his death. In 1972, Bill Tara, who had been managing the macrobiotic natural food company Erewhon in the U.S.A., settled in London and started activity from his home. In 1974 he and Peter Bradford set up Sunwheel Foods. By 1976, they had sufficient support to found the Community Health Foundation, and rent a large five story Victorian school in Old Street, where it is today. In 1981 Bill Tara returned to the States to direct the Kushi Institute and Denny Waxman came to London to organise the Community Health Foundation for two years. Since then it has been run first by Jon Sandifer and now by Simon Brown, who have both developed the activities of the Centre with considerable success.

In Florence there is a good macrobiotic restaurant, Santommasio, in Via Romana. There are centres in Turin, Genoa, Milan, Pesara and groups in several other cities in Italy.

With the emerging of new macrobiotic centres in the USSR and Eastern Europe and the opening of the new home for the Kushi Institute in Becket a new era seems to be opening out for macrobiotics. A list of some of the macrobiotic centres and institutes in Europe will be found at the end of the book under the heading, "Useful addresses".

Chapter 6

MACROBIOTICS - A WIDER VIEW

by Hugh Faulkner

"One should not walk through the world wearing blinkers."
Albert Einstein

Macrobiotics is at a crossroads today. What does it mean to its followers? For some of us it has provided a lifeline when orthodox medicine offered no hope, or an effective system of prevention. For others it is a retreat from modern Western civilisation, a protest against the worst excesses of consumerism, against the destruction of the environment for financial gain, against violence and war. For others yet again it is the "Journey to the East" which the "flower people" followed in the sixties. They happily embrace traditional Japanese philosophy, perhaps the Buddhist religion, Japanese customs and even dress. But others, less concerned with the East, appear to be simply seeking a life as close to nature as possible, growing their own food organically, making their own soya derivatives, baking their own bread, and perhaps making their own clothes. Some reject Western science and medicine completely, and turn to magic and mysticism, showing little concern or responsibility for the wider society, and seemingly engrossed only with the salvation of themselves and their immediate companions. Others seem to be making macrobiotics a substitute for religion. We are in no position to sneer at such approaches. We share much of the desire to reject the consumeristic society and also seek to live as close to nature as we can. But surely this is not enough.

We all have a responsibility to work with others - for peace and for a world freed from ruthless financial exploitation. That Marian and I are not alone in this belief became clear at the last meetings of the International Macrobiotic Assembly in Berlin in November, 1990, and Kiental in November 1991, attended mainly by people active in some sphere of macrobiotics.

Perhaps those of us who have come to macrobiotics with an "incurable" life- threatening illness can be expected to have a different perspective. We are not necessarily travellers on the "journey to the East" or live in a rural commune. We have not all rejected Western science and medicine - though we may have many criticisms and reservations. We are profoundly grateful for the help we have received, but still ask: "Where is macrobiotics going?" In the foreseeable future only a minority of citizens in any Western country will seek to join "the journey to the East" or be attracted to rural communes. They will remain a relatively select in-group - for the most part middle-class. This is surely not what George Ohsawa dreamed of, and I am convinced that Michio Kushi has far wider plans for the new centre at Becket. Macrobiotics faces a major challenge - but also a great opportunity. In reviving traditional Japanese medicine George Ohsawa stumbled upon lessons of supreme importance and relevance to Western society today. In no country is this yet realised - and perhaps not always fully in macrobiotic circles.

If macrobiotics fails to go forward it will decline - or at best stagnate. It has to find new ways of continuing the dialogue between macrobiotics, traditional Eastern medicine and Western medicine. Inevitably Western doctors - and their patients - will ask, "Does it work?" and despite many anecdotal accounts of "miracle cures", macrobiotics has so far failed to provide the evidence that could satisfy Western medical science. Kaptchuk suggests that perhaps some such evidence already exists. After the victory of the communists in China in 1949, the leadership decided to take a fresh look at traditional Chinese medicine. It appears that during the fifties thousands of trials and experiments were carried out.

In 1958 the Chinese communist party became convinced that traditional medicine worked in practice, and despite the Party's lack of success in the political and economic fields, it was not necessarily wrong in this. The government decided to give traditional and modern Western medicine equal rights - often in the same hospital. Patients were offered the choice of which system to consult. I do not know if this continues today. Perhaps with the enthusiasm for a consumer orientated market displayed by the present leadership, the pendulum will have swung back in favour of Western medicine. Yet the reports of these clinical studies should still exist, even if expressed in terms and methodology completely foreign to Western medicine, and could well be extremely informative. "There is hardly a field in all of historical scholarship of which we know so little as the development of Chinese medical thought."[1]

This probably applies equally to Japanese traditional medicine, although a growing interest in acupuncture and shiatsu in the West has led to what seems too often to be a superficial study of Ki (or in the Chinese form Ch'i) and the meridians or "energetic circuits" on which acupuncture, shiatsu and moxibustion are based. Moxibustion involves applying heat at the acupuncture points. The heat is produced by igniting mugwort (artemesia vulgaris) which can be purchased in already prepared sticks. Many unsuccessful attempts have been made in the West to detect some kind of anatomical structure involved, or define some measurable magnetic force. This is surely a potentially fruitful field for co-operative research into the vast literature on Eastern medicine, so far mostly in Chinese or Japanese. But traditional Eastern medicine has far more to offer than acupuncture and shiatsu, useful as these techniques are. Macrobiotics has inherited this approach and is applying it in day to day practice.

1 Porkert, M. *The Theoretical Foundations of Chinese Medicine. (see foreword by Nathan Sivin.)*

Much of this Eastern thinking is highly relevant to the problems facing health care today. In the Taoist approach, life consists of two forces, Yin and Yang, dialectically opposed and in constant motion. Each individual is unique and cannot be seen as an entity separate from his total environment. Ill- health is seen as an imbalance between the individual and nature. Western medicine on the other hand concentrates on the disease and tries to probe it at every level including cellular and molecular. This approach developed from the newtonian cartesian science which saw the human body as an extremely complex machine, is responsible for the very real technological advances in recent years. Unfortunately it too often fails to see the individual patient as a whole - as a unique organic being, in his social, emotional and physical setting. Marxists have frequently pointed this out, and it would be interesting to promote discussion between macrobiotics and biologists who have used the approach of dialectical materialism in their work.[2]

I am not competent to discuss the recent advances of research in physics and allied disciplines, and I have only the haziest notions of relativity and quantum mechanics. However even a casual reading of some books and articles on popular science suggests that much of the medical science I was taught 50 years ago is probably incompatible with recent research, and that some of the concepts of Eastern medicine and macrobiotics begin to seem less improbable.

A profound crisis is developing in health care in Europe and North America. Medicine based on high powered sophisticated technology is producing steadily soaring costs, while, at the same time, increasing numbers of people are becoming aware of the shortcomings of our health care systems and their conceptual framework.[3]

A new global view of society is developing rapidly, in which political, economic, social and environmental factors are

2 Levins, Richard and Lewontin, Richard. *The Dialectical Biologist.*
3 Dossey, L. *Space, Time and Medicine.*

intimately interwoven. Western medical science, with its emphasis on high technology, with the exclusion of disease prevention and health promotion, risks being left behind.

Has macrobiotics a world view? In his lectures Michio Kushi implies that it has. But some of our friends in macrobiotics seem reluctant to admit it, and appear to see only dangers if macrobiotics enters the wider political arena. Yet many of our aims are already political - clean air, pure water, wholesome uncontaminated food, an environment free from violence, a world without war - these cannot be realised without political action. The new objectives of the International Macrobiotic Assembly accept this challenge and represent an important step forward for macrobiotics:

1. To provide a forum for discussion of macrobiotic ideas and practice.
2. To evolve projects at an international level relevant to macrobiotic activity.
3. To collaborate in joint projects with other organisations in social action in the field of health and ecology.
4. To provide networking and support for macrobiotic activists and Organisations in each country.
5. To stimulate and support the growth of macrobiotic activities in countries and areas where they are not yet developed.

Today there is a growing consensus on what constitutes a healthy diet. Sir Richard Doll, ex Regius Professor of medicine at Oxford, summed it up in his Harveian Oration as long ago as 1982: "Whether the object is to avoid cancer, coronary heart disease, hypertension, diabetes, diverticular disease, duodenal ulcer or constipation, there is broad agreement among research workers that the type of diet that is least likely to cause disease is one that provides a high proportion of calories, in whole grain cereals, vegetables and fruit, provides most of its animal protein in fish and poultry, limits the intake of fats, and, if oils are to be used, gives preference to liquid vegetable oils, includes very few dairy products, eggs, and little refined sugar."[4] It is remarkable how close this is to a macrobiotic diet.

Four years later in 1984, the British Medical Association - not always in the vanguard of progress - said in a report by its Board of Science and Education:- "The Ministry of Agriculture, Fisheries and Food will wish to support the food industry... Present policies artificially raise consumption of either potentially harmful products, such as sugar, whole fat milk and butter, or less healthy products such as white bread."[5]

Some Kushi institutes and macrobiotic centres are beginning to invite speakers from other organisations and disciplines. For example John Robbins, author of the best seller "Diet for a New America", gave the keynote lecture at the 1990 Macrobiotic Summer Conference at Amherst, Boston, which aroused a great deal of interest and discussion amongst the participants. I hope this example will be followed in other places, and speakers will be invited from the many areas of common interest - ecology, pollution, traffic, pesticides, organic agriculture, food additives, bird and animal sanctuaries, health promotion and prevention of illness, recent advances in scientific research - particularly in psychoneurology and immunology.

Despite their immense power, the multinationals are extremely sensitive to public opinion and any adverse criticism which can directly affect sales. This needs to be carried out on a mass scale, and will demand co-operation with other like-minded organisations and individuals. Of course this is "dabbling in politics", but we must never forget that any effective action is "political" whether we like it or not. Even passivity is political action - in support of the status quo.

4 Cannon, G. *The Politics of Food.*
5 Cannon, G. Ibid.

Once we convince any government of the political necessity to do something about these issues - food, ecology, and pollution - mass pressure could bring about legislation which could greatly reduce if not abolish the worst of the abuses. Such changes will not come about spontaneously. The politicians have got to be told that these new policies are vote-winners. In the development of mass pressure we all have a part to play, and macrobiotics can have an important role. We cannot afford to stand aside.

We have met few women in a leading role in macrobiotics - with the obvious exceptions of Aveline Kushi and Shizuko Yamamoto in New York. Yet macrobiotic counselling seems to be ideally suited to the special skills and gifts of women, whose activities should surely not be solely confined to the kitchen, however essential and exciting the art of macrobiotic cooking may be. As men took control of the medical establishment in the West, women were gradually excluded from their traditional roles in healing. Midwives were replaced by obstetricians, medical cookery and herbalism were absorbed in the academic fields of pharmacy, dietetics and botany - dominated mainly by men. Midwives who had been doctors and teachers of other women, became assistants to obstetricians and only worked on their own with the very poor, who could not afford a doctor. Women became "ancillaries" - in ancient Greece the handmaidens to the Gods. As the male expert, legitimised by regulations and medical schools which excluded women, took over all organised health care, women lost control over their own health. As early as 1666 Margaret Cavendish wrote: "For though the Muses, Graces and Sciences are all of feminine gender, yet they were more esteemed in former ages than they are now; nay, could it be done handsomely, they would turn them all from Females into Males, so great is grown the self-conceit of the Masculine, and the disregard of the Female Sex". Let us determine that macrobiotics will restore women to a leading role in health care.

In conclusion, I am convinced that a macrobiotic diet and life-style can make most of us healthier and help to prevent many diseases. It may well prolong life, and if it does not add 'years to life' it can certainly add 'life to years'. We need properly conducted clinical trials on the effect of a macrobiotic regime on various types of established chronic illness, and long term trials of its role in prevention and health promotion. The unfortunate experience of the Bristol Centre teaches us that such research must be very carefully planned at every stage. The anecdotal evidence I and many others have provided won't convince many of my medical colleagues.

From my own personal experience it is clear that in cases where orthodox medicine can offer no effective treatment a percentage of patients can recover. I firmly believe that we can directly influence this result by adopting a macrobiotic way of life - a positive outlook, a healthy diet, physical and mental activity, fresh air, pure water, getting as close to nature as we can - and above all love and hope! If our book can help others to realise this objective it will have achieved its aim.

Chapter 7

WHAT TO EXPECT FROM A MACROBIOTIC DIET

by Simon Brown

This chapter is solely based on my experience in helping thousands of people start a macrobiotic diet through individual advice, and introductory courses. I have been fortunate in keeping in contact with many of these people and listening to their experiences.

There is currently no scientific evidence to suggest people will recover from serious illness on a macrobiotic diet. The natural role of macrobiotics is in preventive medicine. However there are enough anecdotal stories such as Hugh Faulkner's to give people a feeling of hope, to open the possibility of beating the odds and making a full recovery. As a result of this, although most people beginning macrobiotics are in good health, people have tried a macrobiotic diet in the face of serious illness. Not all of these people have had the same success as Hugh Faulkner, however it has often been observed by close relatives that they experienced a better quality of life, and in some cases they have told me that their husband or wife died very peacefully.

I have been very fortunate to know Hugh Faulkner and other people in a similar situation as this has shown me how much someone can improve the quality of their life. For many of these people it is the day to day process of living that really counts.

In the end the only way to find out if macrobiotics is going to work for each person is to try it. Most people are in a position to decide whether it will help after six weeks of accurately following their macrobiotic diet.

The initial improvements a macrobiotic counsellor will be looking for are an increase in energy, a full night's sleep, a good appetite, regular bowel movements, greater concentration, and greater emotional stability. In my experience it is realistic to see an improvement in some of these measures of health within six weeks.

For many people starting a macrobiotic diet requires major changes to their diet. Occasionally these changes result in temporary symptoms. This can include constipation, diarrhoea, headaches or tiredness. These usually disappear within the first ten days. However, it is worth seeking advice as many of the symptoms can be simply helped with a temporary adjustment to the diet.

The benefits of eating a macrobiotic diet are unique to each person. Most commonly reported are: an increase in energy, a reduction in the intensity and incidence of common aches and pains, a more comfortable weight, skin that looks and feels more healthy, a greater ability to relax, an improvement in memory and clearer thinking. Some people notice significant improvements after a few days, whereas for others it may be 3 months.

People are often justifiably concerned about the taste of what is often a completely different diet. This largely depends on what was eaten before. Someone used to a highly seasoned diet with large quantities of sugar, salt or spices will often find that a macrobiotic diet tastes bland initially. Eating a relatively simple diet often allows the taste senses to adjust and become more sensitive so that a simple vegetable has a satisfying taste. This process is similar to letting your eyes adjust after being exposed to bright sunlight or your ears adjust after going to a loud concert. Most people find they enjoy most of the macrobiotic tastes within 3 months. People find meat the easiest food to replace with healthier alternatives. Refined sugar often proves to be the most difficult. Once you start to read food labels it's shocking to find how many common foods contain added refined sugar.

Someone who already enjoys eating a vegetarian diet, a whole food diet or a diet high in fresh vegetables, usually likes the tastes of a macrobiotic diet straight away. It often provides a greater variety of tastes and many new recipe ideas. Perhaps the most unusual tastes are those of the seaweeds and the fermented foods like miso, shoyu and natto. As with most foods, it is often a case of acquiring the taste for these foods, and there are many creative ways in which these tastes can be altered. In the end, however, the macrobiotic diet does not rely on any one particular ingredient and can be adapted to suit personal tastes. Initially anyone starting a different diet, learning to use new foods and trying new ways of cooking will inevitably spend more time in the kitchen. Once enough recipes to form a balanced diet have been learnt and you are familiar with the basic techniques of preparing macrobiotic foods, it becomes easier to organise your time efficiently. The recipes for ten days to get started are put together in such a way as to use anyone's time efficiently. A complete macrobiotic meal can be created in one and a half hours, including miso soup, grains, beans, two vegetable dishes and dessert. On other days, quick cooking foods such as noodles, couscous, vegetables, tofu, fish or macrobiotic convenience foods can be used to create a meal in 20 minutes.

Starting a macrobiotic diet will be an adventure and a challenge. It requires a certain amount of time and effort to learn and to do properly. Once mastered, the principles and ideas can be applied to any situation and even to the most hectic lifestyle.

Chapter 8

DOES MACROBIOTICS PROVIDE ENOUGH NUTRIENTS?

by Simon Brown

People beginning a macrobiotic diet often ask about where their protein, calcium and iron will come from. This is largely because it is assumed that protein and iron come from meat and calcium from diary food.

Numerous research projects have shown that this is not the case and yet the myth still persists.

PROTEIN

The requirements for protein are given as a percentage of our total calorie intake. Recommendations range from 2½% to 8%. The World Health Organisation recommends a minimum requirement of 32 grams of protein each day for a 150 pound man, which equates to 4½% of calorific value of the food eaten.

Surprisingly, it is impossible to design a palatable diet of natural foods that will not meet these requirements. In fact Nathan Pritikin, a leading American nutrition expert found it practically impossible to get below 9%. A lower figure would only be achieved by using 'empty calories' such as refined sugar.

In a macrobiotic diet protein deficiency is the last thing to worry about. There is protein in high quantities in nearly all the foods shown overleaf:

The Department of Health dietary reference values quote an estimated average protein requirement of 44.4 g per day for an adult male (19-49 years old) and 36.0 g per day for an adult female (19-49 years old).

	g / 100g
GRAINS	
Brown Rice (Boiled)	02.6
Corn on the Cob (Boiled)	04.1
Oat meal (Raw)	12.4
Wholemeal Flower	13.2
Wholemeal Bread	08.8
VEGETABLES	
Broccoli Tops (Boiled)	03.1
Brussels Sprouts (Boiled)	02.8
Cabbage (Raw)	02.8
Kale (Boiled)	01.5
Leek (Boiled)	01.8
Parsley (Raw)	05.2
Peas (Boiled)	05.0
Radishes (Raw)	01.0
Shiitake Mushrooms (Boiled)	09.5
Watercress (Raw)	02.9
SEA VEGETABLES	
Arame (Dried)	06.0
Nori (Dried)	22.2
BEANS	
Butter beans (Boiled)	07.1
Chickpeas (Boiled)	08.0
Lentils (Boiled)	07.6
Soya beans (Boiled)	10.5
Split peas (Boiled)	08.3
SOYA PRODUCTS	
Miso	11.8
Natto	17.7
Tempeh	19.0
Tofu	07.4
FISH	
Cod (Poached)	20.9
Haddock (Steamed)	2.8
Herring (Grilled)	20.4
Plaice (Fried in bread crumbs)	18.0

	g/ 100g
Mackerel (Fried)	21.5
Mussels (Boiled)	17.3
Salmon (Steamed)	20.1
Trout (Steamed)	23.5
Whitebait (Fried)	19.5
SEEDS	
Pumpkin	25.0
Sesame	25.0
Sunflower	21.0
NUTS	
Almonds	16.9
Peanuts (Roasted)	24.3
Walnuts	10.6
FRUIT	
Apples (Raw)	00.3
Raisins (Dried)	01.1
DAIRY FOOD	
Butter	00.4
Cheese cheddar	26.0
Cheese cottage	13.6
Egg (Boiled)	12.3
Milk fresh skimmed	03.4
Milk fresh whole	03.3
Yogurt natural low fat	05.0
MEAT	
Bacon (Fried)	24.1
Beef (Minced and stewed)	23.1
Beef steak (Grilled)	27.3
Chicken (Roasted)	24.8
Curried meat	09.6
Irish stew	05.2
Lamb chops (Grilled)	23.5
Shepherds Pie	07.6
HUMAN BREAST MILK	
Human milk mature	01.3

The Composition of Foods. Ministry of Agriculture Fisheries and Food, and Medical Research Council. (Published by H.M.S.O.) and U.S. Department of Agriculture.

In nature any food that has to grow, whether a vegetable, bean or grain will contain protein. As a macrobiotic diet is predominantly made up of these whole 'living' foods, supplemented with fish, it would be harder to become protein deficient than with many other more common styles of eating. For example, people would be much more likely to become protein deficient eating a junk food diet high in sugary foods such as sweets, soft drinks, biscuits, alcohol, fatty foods, greasy foods, and highly processed or refined foods such as white bread.There has been some debate over whether protein from meat is of a higher quality. However leading medical opinion no longer supports this view, as reported in the Lancet in 1959, and the Journal of the American Dietetic Association in 1973.

It is also important to remember that nothing is completely excluded from a macrobiotic diet. In certain cases where someone requires an unusually high level of protein, or for a young child, or a pregnant mother it may be sensible to include more forms of protein rich food such as fish. These choices depend on each individual in his own unique circumstance.

IRON

Low iron levels lead to anaemia resulting in a tired listless condition, dizziness and depression. External signs are a pale colour on the inner lower eyelids, pale lips or pale finger nails. As with protein, it has often been assumed that meat is the best source or iron, however this is a myth that does not stand up to scrutiny. Many green leafy vegetables have three times more iron per calorie than red meat.

A sirloin steak has 1.9 milligrams per 100 calories whereas turnip greens have 6 milligrams per 100 calories. In fact the China project showed that people eating very little animal food had excellent iron counts.

The Department of Health dietary reference values quote an estimated average requirement of iron of 6.7 mg per day for an adult male (19-49 years old) and 11.4 mg per day for an adult female (19-49 years old).

	mg / 100g
GRAINS	
Brown Rice (Boiled)	00.50
Corn on the Cob (Boiled)	00.90
Oat meal (Raw)	04.10
Wholemeal Flour	04.00
Wholemeal Bread	02.50
VEGETABLES	
Broccoli Tops (Boiled)	01.00
Brussels Sprouts (Boiled)	00.50
Cabbage (Raw)	00.60
Kale (Boiled)	00.90
Leek (Boiled)	02.00
Parsley (Raw)	08.00
Peas (Boiled)	01.50
Radishes (Raw)	01.90
Shiitake Mushrooms (Boiled)	00.44
Watercress (Raw)	01.60
SEA VEGETABLES	
Arame (Dried)	12.00
Hiziki (Dried)	29.00
Kombu (Soaked)	06.10
Nori (Dried)	28.30
BEANS	
Butter beans (Boiled)	01.70
Chickpeas (Boiled)	03.10
Lentils (Boiled)	02.40
Split peas (Boiled)	01.70
SOYA PRODUCTS	
Miso	02.74
Natto	08.60
Tempeh	02.26
Tofu	01.20

	mg / 100g
FISH	
Cockles	26.00
Cod (Poached)	00.30
Haddock (Steamed)	00.70
Herring (Grilled)	01.00
Plaice (Fried in bread crumbs)	00.80
Mackerel (Fried)	01.20
Mussels (Boiled)	07.70
Salmon (Steamed)	00.80
Trout (Steamed)	01.00
Whitebait (Fried)	05.10
SEEDS	
Pumpkin	15.00
Sesame	07.50
Sunflower	06.70
NUTS	
Almonds	04.20
Chestnuts (Dried)	03.30
Peanuts (Roasted)	02.00
Walnuts	02.40
FRUIT	
Apples (Raw)	00.30
Peaches (Steamed)	02.50
Raisins (Dried)	01.60
DAIRY FOOD	
Butter	00.16
Cheese cheddar	00.40
Cheese cottage	00.10
Egg (Boiled)	02.00
Milk fresh skimmed	00.05
Milk fresh whole	00.50
Yogurt natural low fat	00.09

	mg / 100g		mg / 100g
MEAT		Irish stew	00.60
Bacon (Fried)	01.30	Lamb chops (Grilled)	01.90
Beef (Minced and stewed)	03.10	Shepherds Pie	01.10
Beef steak (Grilled)	03.40		
Chicken (Roasted)	00.80	HUMAN BREAST MILK	
Curried meat	02.90	Human milk mature	00.07

The Composition of Foods. Ministry of Agriculture Fisheries and Food, and Medical Research Council. (Published by H.M.S.O.) and U.S. Department of Agriculture.

The China project shows that a macrobiotic style diet will lead to excellent iron levels, however at times of high demands such as pregnancy or of blood loss from excessive menstrual flow it may be necessary to increase the intake of iron.Within a typical macrobiotic diet a handful of watercress or parsley steamed or sauteed in sesame oil with dulse seaweed eaten daily will often help. Try raw fresh tuna fish (Japanese sashimi style) if you feel adventurous, otherwise increase the intake of fish generally.

CALCIUM

It is normally assumed that the best source of calcium is dairy foods. Although dairy foods are high in calcium many other foods contain similar concentrations of calcium. In addition there is a price to pay when relying on dairy foods for calcium. Unfortunately dairy foods are very high in saturated fats - the very thing that people like the WHO are recommending people reduce to improve their health. In fact the China Health Project found that a more than adequate supply of calcium could be derived from a diet with no dairy food. Most people eating a macrobiotic diet eat very little or no dairy food. Their calcium will come from vegetables, sea vegetables, fish, tofu, nuts, and seeds.

The Department of Health dietary reference values quote an estimated average requirement of calcium of 525 mg per day for an adult.

	mg / 100g
GRAINS	
Oat meal (Raw)	053
Rye (Whole germ)	038
Wholemeal bread	023
VEGETABLES	
Broccoli Tops (Boiled)	114
Chinese leaves	076
Kale (Boiled)	072
Parsley (Raw)	330
Spring Onion	140
Swede (Boiled)	059
Turnip Greens (Boiled)	137
Watercress (Raw)	220
SEA VEGETABLES	
Arame (Dried)	1170
Hiziki (Dried)	1400
Kombu (Soaked)	955
Nori (Dried)	434
BEANS	
Chickpeas (Boiled)	064
Haricot (Boiled)	065
Soya (Boiled)	068
SOYA PRODUCTS	
Miso	066
Natto	217
Tempeh	093
Tofu	507
FISH	
Cod (Poached)	029
Haddock (Steamed)	055
Herring (Grilled)	039
Mackerel (Fried)	028
Mussels (Boiled)	200
Salmon (Steamed)	029
Whitebait (Fried)	860
SEEDS	
Sesame	137
Sunflower	117
NUTS	
Almonds	250
Peanuts	061
Walnuts	061
DAIRY FOOD	
Butter	015
Cheese cheddar	800
Cheese cottage	060
Egg (Boiled)	059
Milk fresh skimmed	120
Milk fresh whole	120
Yogurt natural low fat	180
MEAT	
Bacon (Fried)	013
Beef (Minced and stewed)	018
Beef steak (Grilled)	007
Chicken (Roasted)	009
Curried meat	033
Irish stew	012
Lamb chops (Grilled)	009
Shepherds Pie	015
HUMAN BREAST MILK	
Human milk mature	034

The Composition of Foods. Ministry of Agriculture Fisheries and Food, and Medical Research Council. (Published by H.M.S.O.) and U.S. Department of Agriculture.

VITAMIN B 12

There has been concern among a few nutritionists that a macrobiotic diet could be lacking in vitamin B 12. A lack of B 12 leads to a condition called pernicious anaemia. B 12 is at present the most recent nutrient to be discovered and there is even some question as to whether foods that show up as having B 12 can actually be digested in a way that the body absorbs B 12. Vitamin B 12 can be found in fermented products such as beer, miso, or tempeh. However anyone who is at all worried about B 12 should eat fish regularly, especially those fish high in B 12. The body stores a few years supply of B 12 in the liver and we therefore do not apparently need B 12 on a constant basis. Pregnant women, and breast feeding mothers have increased demands for B 12 and young children may not yet have built up a reserve of B 12.

The Department of Health dietary reference values quote an estimated average requirement of 0.4µg per day for 1-3 year olds, 0.7 µg per day for 4-6 year olds, 0.8 µg per day for 7-10 year olds, 1.0 µg per day for 11-14 year olds, and 1.25 µg per day for anyone over 15 years of age.

	µg / 100g
SOYA PRODUCTS	
Miso	00.21
Tempeh	00.84
FISH	
Cod (Poached)	02.00
Haddock (Steamed)	01.00
Herring (Grilled)	11.00
Plaice (Fried in bread crumbs)	01.00
Mackerel (Fried)	12.00
Oysters (Raw)	15.00
Salmon (Steamed)	06.00
BEERS	
Strong ale	00.37
Pale ale	00.14
Draught bitter	00.17
DAIRY FOOD	
Butter	Trace
Cheese cheddar	01.50

	µg / 100g
Cheese cottage	00.50
Egg (Boiled)	01.70
Milk fresh skimmed	00.30
Milk fresh whole	00.30
Yogurt natural low fat	Trace
MEAT	
Bacon (Fried)	Trace
Beef (Minced and stewed)	02.00
Beef steak (Grilled)	02.00
Chicken (Roasted)	Trace
Curried meat	01.00
Irish stew	01.00
Lamb chops (Grilled)	02.00
Shepherd's Pie	01.00
HUMAN BREAST MILK	
Human milk mature	Trace

The Composition of Foods. Ministry of Agriculture Fisheries and Food, and Medical Research Council. (Published by H.M.S.O.) and U.S. Department of Agriculture.

VITAMIN D

Vitamin D is absorbed through sunlight or certain foods. Although in many countries sufficient vitamin D may be obtained solely from sunlight, in a country like Britain where during the winter months there are long periods of cloud cover, dietary sources are important.

Typical dietary sources are dairy foods , eggs, liver, and fish. In general meat only contains trace elements of vitamin D. In a macrobiotic diet fish and sunlight would be the primary sources of vitamin D. The greater your exposure to sunlight the less fish you require. The fish with high levels of vitamin D are listed below.

	µg / 100g
Cod roe	02.0
Herring (grilled)	25.0
Kipper (baked)	25.0
Mackerel (fried)	21.1

Most other fish contain trace elements.

The Composition of Foods. Ministry of Agriculture Fisheries and Food, and Medical Research Council. (Published by H.M.S.O.) and U.S. Department of Agriculture.

Chapter 9

GETTING STARTED

by Simon Brown

The easiest way to learn macrobiotic cooking is to attend a macrobiotic cooking course. If you have particular concerns about your health it is also recommended you see a macrobiotic counsellor who will adapt the macrobiotic diet to suit your own requirements. When neither of these is available, it is also possible to learn from a book or video. I would suggest using two or three books by different authors. There are limitations in this approach as books communicating through written word tend to appear rigid and generalised. At best they can point someone in a new direction and provide general advice, but are unable to help each person with his or her own unique individual needs. In my experience, contact with other people eating macrobiotically, macrobiotic cooks or macrobiotic counsellors is important in the first year. It will certainly help avoid unnecessary mistakes and provide essential help in making what for most people is one of the biggest changes to their lives.

Until recently, there were very few examples of human beings dramatically changing their diet in this way, particularly over such a short time. So it is well worth getting help from people who have already made the changes and do it well. In the story of his introduction to macrobiotics, Hugh Faulkner talks about having a macrobiotic counselling session at the Community Health Foundation. This takes the form of sitting down with an experienced macrobiotic practitioner who will tailor the macrobiotic diet to suit each person's needs. Talking to a macrobiotic counsellor is most useful for anyone who is eating macrobiotically because he or she wants to improve a health problem, or for someone who is already eating macrobiotically and has special considerations such as pregnancy, weaning babies or feeding young children.

The macrobiotic counsellor will be interested in what the person wants to change about his or her health and then take a full account of his or her current situation. This would typically include energy levels, ability to get a full night's sleep, appetite, any cravings for certain foods, any digestive problems, frequency of bowel movements, ability to concentrate, memory, emotional state , how they feel under stress and any aches or pains. In addition a macrobiotic counsellor will often be interested in what the person currently eats, his or her lifestyle, and career. A macrobiotic counsellor will also be trained in 'oriental diagnosis' which is a subjective form of a diagnosis traditionally used in the Orient. It simply looks at the condition of the parts of the outside of the body that can reflect the health of the inside. For example, whether the palms of a persons's hands are wet or dry, whether their lips are pale, or the colour of the skin below their eyes will all help to gain an impression of what kind of diet someone needs.

By putting everything together a macrobiotic counsellor will have a picture of how someone could benefit from macrobiotics and how he or she could best start. He then designs a diet to eat for the first one to three months. Most macrobiotic counsellors encourage the person to keep in touch with them by telephone, as there is often an element of trial and error in the early stages. In any case, people often forget important questions or need help in the first few weeks of their new way of eating. It is always useful to have someone who knows you, your history and what you are eating to talk to if problems occur. At the time of writing a macrobiotic consultation at the Community Health Foundation costs £30-00 with no extra charge for subsequent telephone conversations.

Normally anyone would only see a macrobiotic counsellor for advice on starting a macrobiotic diet. Macrobiotic counsellors are not qualified to give medical advice and seeing a qualified doctor is always recommended.

At the end of an appointment with a macrobiotic counsellor, anyone should have a clear idea of how to get started, have all the recipes he or she needs to suit his or her own requirements and someone he can talk to as he begins his new adventure. An introductory cooking course would teach the basic cooking techniques, present the ingredients and teach you how to make the most important dishes. The value of a cooking course is in actually being able to see how a dish is made, cook the dish yourself with guidance and then know how it should taste. Cooking courses are also a natural place to discuss difficulties in starting macrobiotics and to get help with cooking tips for each person's situation.

People often ask whether they should change straight to a macrobiotic diet. Although I know people who, after a cooking course rushed home with their new macrobiotic foods, threw out all their old foods and began eating macrobiotically straight away, many people choose to ease into a macrobiotic diet over several weeks. Either way is beneficial as long as it gets the person to the point where he can try eating macrobiotically properly. As with any way of eating it is essential to cook with enough variety of ingredients and cooking methods to get all the nutrients required. This therefore places an unusual demand on someone beginning macrobiotic cooking as he needs to learn enough recipes to enjoy that variety at the beginning.

A common mistake is to learn a few recipes, become familiar and confident with them and then cook them over and over again. Not only is it boring after a while but also not particularly healthy. Wherever possible I would suggest learning at least three soup recipes, six grain recipes, twelve vegetable recipes, six bean recipes, six recipes using bean products (tofu or tempeh) knowing how to use five different sea vegetables, three dessert recipes, being able to make four types of snacks, and two hot drinks within the first four weeks of starting a macrobiotic diet.

It is often easiest to start a macrobiotic diet gradually by learning new recipes every day until you have enough to begin a proper macrobiotic diet with confidence. The only risk is that this transition can go on indefinitely unless you set yourself a date to work towards. I always suggest to people starting a macrobiotic diet to simply take one day at a time. Try not to worry about whether you will grow to like all the foods, if you can cope with the changes or how to fit it into your lifestyle. Simply concentrating on each meal as you cook it is the best you can do to make macrobiotics a successful part of your life. Many of the problems you think you may have disappear before you get to them. People often start macrobiotics full of enthusiasm and decide never to have any meat, dairy food or sugar. Then the inevitable happens and they have something with sugar in it or some dairy food. They often interpret this as some kind of failure or weakness and begin to feel guilty about it. This is made worse if they have already told their friends of their new diet. The more healthy attitude is to just concentrate on each meal. No-one can change the past, and if you ate something you wished you had not, the best anyone can do is learn from the experience. See if you can notice any effects from eating that food, and try to identify why you wanted to eat it. The aim is to move forward to each meal positively. To be free from worries and concerns, and fully prepared to make an excellent macrobiotic meal. The most unhealthy scenario is where someone is eating a much more healthy diet but plagued with guilt and worry about eating foods he thinks are now unhealthy and wishes he could stop eating.

Once anyone feels he is ready to just eat macrobiotically, I suggest trying to follow the macrobiotic recommendations accurately and carefully for six weeks. For most people this is enough time to notice beneficial changes in their health and get used to the new ingredients. After this you are in a good position to assess the value of macrobiotic foods and see how they can help you. It may be that at this time some people feel it is not for them. However, unless you try it , it is impossible to know. As time goes by, the diet can be relaxed more as the health improves, as was the case for Hugh Faulkner.

Starting a macrobiotic diet is always a learning process where ideally someone with experience can help each person as they become confident and competent at feeding themselves healthy macrobiotic foods. However this is only the beginning. As time goes by, each person can adapt and create his own version of macrobiotics based on what fits into his lifestyle and what makes him feel good. Once someone is familiar with the basic principles and has mastered the cooking techniques, he can easily create and make up his own new recipes. Some people who eat macrobiotically will use any recipe book, such as a French gourmet cookbook, and use it to design their own macrobiotic versions of the dishes. Eventually people eating macrobiotically create their own macrobiotic kitchen, not only stocked with all the macrobiotic ingredients but also with beans soaking, ready made food in the fridge and convenience foods ready for emergencies. Initially starting macrobiotics can seem quite expensive. Introductory courses start at about £70-00 for a weekend and an appointment with a macrobiotic counsellor £30-00. In addition when starting, most people have to stock their kitchen from scratch. Some of the more expensive ingredients like seaweeds, miso, shoyu, umeboshi plums, kuzu and vinegars will last a long time and are cheaper bought in bulk. Once established, a macrobiotic diet tends to be similar in cost to an average diet and can be made even cheaper. The staple products (grains, beans and vegetables) are all relatively cheap.

George Ohsawa was committed to the idea of 'Non Credo'. Basically do not believe anything. To him it was essential that each person discovered macrobiotics for himself and learnt through his own experience. He did not want anyone to believe his opinions but to use them to initiate his own research and experimentation. Over the last nine years, the people I have met who get the most out of macrobiotics are those who have made it their own. They experimented, made mistakes, and adapted. Each time they knew more about themselves and became more aware of their food. This approach becomes a lifetime learning process in which each person learns how to use food as a positive influence on his life. People eat all the time anyway. It is simply being more aware of what you are eating and being able to make the best choices.

VARIETY

Variety is important. Everyone needs wide variety of ingredients to get all the carbohydrates, proteins, fats, vitamins and minerals for health. However, the way these foods are cooked make a difference to which nutrients become most digestible and which nutrients are altered during the cooking process. For example, when one carrot is boiled in a little water for half an hour and another boiled for one minute, the carrot which has been boiled longer will taste sweeter and richer. Certain nutrients have become more digestible by cooking the carrot for so long. The other carrot will taste sharper, fresher and be more crunchy. This carrot will still retain the fragile nutrients such as vitamins, that are changed during longer cooking. Other nutrients will not be as digestible and readily absorbed into the blood as the longer cooked carrot. Similarly, if one carrot is boiled and the other baked, the fat in the baked carrot will be more digestible and easier to absorb. The amount of oil soluble and water soluble vitamins in the carrot will change as it is boiled or fried. When the carrot is steamed it is cooked at a higher temperature but not immersed in water where some nutrients will dissolve into the water. Essentially this means that each cooking style will influence what is digested and absorbed from the food.

So not only is it important to have a variety of ingredients, but also to use many different styles of cooking. To get every nutrient possible out of carrots over a period of time they would need to be boiled quickly, stewed, baked, steamed fried and made into soups.

People often ask why those eating macrobiotically do not eat more raw vegetables. Although raw vegetables are a natural part of a macrobiotic diet, particularly in the summer, it is only one way of preparing food. They may still contain all the nutrients in their natural form, but if these nutrients are less digestible than a lightly cooked vegetable, in the end it will not be possible to absorb as much nutrition from the raw vegetable. The real issue is not only which nutrients the food contains but how digestible they are, how much of the food actually gets into the body and which stored nutrients are lost from the body when it tries to digest certain foods.

Chapter 10

RECIPES

by Simon Brown & Bob Lloyd

INTRODUCTION

The following recipes have been designed to introduce a range of new recipes in such a way that illustrates how to; plan ahead, cook quantities to last for more than one meal, and save time. Once the ten days have been completed, the same sequence may be repeated or the most appropriate recipes taken and used more often. For example, in hot weather, after the first ten days the lighter dishes would need to be emphasised. Conversely in cold weather the dishes that take longer to cook need a greater emphasis. It is strongly recommended that anyone beginning macrobiotics from this book takes a macrobiotic cooking course and buys a complete recipe book for a greater range of recipes.

DAY ONE

- **BREAKFAST**
  PORRIDGE OATS
  ROASTED SUNFLOWER SEEDS
  BARLEY MALT (OPTIONAL)
  BANCHA TEA

PORRIDGE OATS

1 cup jumbo oatflakes
2 1/2 cups cold water
1 pinch sea salt

Mix oats with water and salt in a saucepan and bring to a gentle boil, stirring from time to time. Place a flame spreader over the heat and simmer, covered for about 15-20 minutes. Serve with the sunflower seeds and, if required, a little barley malt.

ROASTED SUNFLOWER SEEDS

It is best to roast a batch to last a week or two and keep them in a sealed jar handy for regular use as snacks and garnishes.

Rinse the seeds in a wire sieve and drain thoroughly but do not dry. Heat a heavy-based frying pan and add the seeds. Stir them with a wooden spoon or spatula to stop them from burning. Keep stirring gently until the seeds are a golden brown colour all over. Transfer to a dish to cool and then place in a jar and seal.

BANCHA TEA

Boil about a pint of water and add a level dessertspoonful of bancha tea twigs. Simmer covered for about 5 minutes, strain and serve. Fast boiling over long periods tends to make the tea bitter so make sure you only boil for a short period. You can use the same twigs several times adding a few extra each time and boiling again.

☐ *PREPARATION FOR THE EVENING MEAL*

Take about a cup of green lentils and pick them through for stones and stalks. This is important! Rinse the lentils in a wire sieve, place in a bowl and cover with water to soak. Green lentils will cook without soaking but they take longer. Other smaller lentils do not require soaking but are still worth picking over in the morning so that you just have to wash and cook them in the evening when you return from work.

■ SNACKS

Bancha tea, rice cakes with peanut butter or sugar-free jam

■ LUNCH

FRIED UDON NOODLES
STEAMED GREENS WITH SAUERKRAUT
SPRING WATER

FRIED UDON NOODLES

1 packet udon wholewheat noodles
2 onions finely sliced
2 carrots cut into matchsticks
Soy sauce
Root ginger
Sesame oil
4 pints water
Finely sliced spring onion

Bring water to the boil in a large saucepan and add the noodles, a few at a time, stirring to avoid sticking. There is no need to add salt as these noodles already contain some. Bring back to the boil and cook until expanded and cooked through. You can tell when they are cooked by breaking one in half. If it is the same colour right through, it is cooked. If not, they will require a little longer. Depending on the make, they usually take about 10-15 minutes. When cooked, drain and rinse in cold water to stop them sticking together. Next, heat some oil in a pan and add the onions. Sauté until soft and translucent before adding the carrots. Continue to sauté for about 3 minutes then place the drained noodles on top of the vegetables. Add a little cold water and cover pan. Simmer until the carrots are just soft then add some soy sauce to taste and, if you wish, some ginger juice. You get the juice by grating the root quite finely and then squeezing it over the noodles so that all the juice comes out. Continue to simmer for a couple of minutes and then serve garnished with the spring onion. You can save some of the noodles in a covered glass container in the refrigerator for the next day if you wish.

STEAMED GREENS WITH SAUERKRAUT

Greens (kale, spring greens, brussel tops etc.)
Sauerkraut

Wash the greens and cut out any thick stems. You can steam them in a little boiling water in a tight covered pan or in a bamboo or metal steamer placed over a pan with boiling water in it. Steam until the leaves have gone a very dark green in colour (usually just 2 or 3 minutes). Meanwhile, slice the stems very finely and steam these separately until soft or use them up in soups. When the greens are cooked, transfer them to a plate and allow them to cool. Drain some sauerkraut, rinsing in cold water if too salty and then add to the greens and mix.

■ SNACKS

ROASTED SEEDS, PEANUTS AND RAISINS

1 cup pumpkin seeds
1 cup sunflower seeds
1 cup peanuts
1 cup raisins

Wash, drain and roast the seeds as described in the breakfast menu. Roast the peanuts in a tin tray in a medium oven until cooked through but not too dark. After about 5 minutes roasting, stir the nuts to give even cooking. Cool the nuts and seeds thoroughly and mix in the raisins. Store in an airtight jar for future use.

■ DINNER

BROWN RICE WITH ROASTED PUMPKIN SEEDS
LENTIL STEW
BOILED CAULIFLOWER AND BROCCOLI
BANCHA TEA

BROWN RICE

2 cups short or medium grain brown rice
3 cups cold water
2 pinches sea salt

Place rice in a large bowl, pan or pressure cooker and add some water. Gently agitate the grains to wash them and then pour off the water. Do this twice more and then place the rice into a wire sieve to drain thoroughly. If pressure cooking, place the rice into the pressure cooker and level out. Add the water by gently pouring round the sides of the pan. Add the salt, cover the pan and bring to pressure. When pressure is up, turn flame to very low and place a flame spreader under the pan. Pressure cook for 45-50 minutes. If the pressure comes down, place pan on a high flame to bring it back and then place on the flame spreader again to continue cooking. You may need to add on a few extra minutes of cooking time to allow for this. If boiling, place the rice in a large, heavy based pan and add the water as described above. Add the salt, cover and bring to a boil (you can hear when it has come to the boil). Turn very low and place a heated flame spreader underneath. Cook for 50 minutes. When the rice has cooked, let the pressure come down naturally and then uncover. Remove rice into a wet wooden bowl or a china or glass dish (using a moistened rice paddle is easiest),spreading the grains out gently with the side of the paddle. Cover with a sushi mat or a clean tea towel. If boiling the rice, turn off the flame when cooked and allow to stand for 5 minutes to allow any stuck grains to loosen on the bottom of the pan. Then proceed as above. Serve garnished with your already roasted pumpkin seeds.

LENTIL STEW

1 cup prepared lentils (see above)
2 onions finely diced
2 stalks celery finely sliced
2 carrots quartered lengthwise and then cut into small dice
1 x 3 inch piece of kombu soaked in a little cold water for 10 minutes then finely sliced
Sea salt
Lemon juice
Some finely chopped parsley for garnish (optional)

Heat a little water or oil if preferred in a large pan and sauté the onions for a couple of minutes. Add the celery, carrots, kombu and lentils in that order and cover with water. Bring to a boil, cover and reduce heat to a gentle simmer. Continue cooking until all the ingredients are soft, adding more water if necessary. (The addition of a bay leaf is very tasty). When cooked, season with the salt and simmer for a further 5 minutes. (DON'T add the salt until the lentils are soft as they may not soften otherwise). Turn off the heat and add some lemon juice to taste. Place in a serving bowl and garnish with the parsley.

BOILED SALAD

1 cup cauliflower florets
1 cup broccoli florets (any extra stems from these Vegetables can be sliced thinly)
Water for boiling
Umeboshi vinegar
Rice vinegar

Cook the vegetables separately in fast boiling water for a short period. You want them to be quite crunchy, not soft. Drain thoroughly, mix together and then make a dressing with some cooking liquid and the vinegars to taste. Toss with the vegetables.

DAY TWO

■ BREAKFAST

SOFT RICE WITH ROASTED SEEDS & UMEBOSHI
YANNOH GRAIN COFFEE

SOFT RICE

1 cup cooked rice
Water
Umeboshi plum
Roasted seeds

Place cooked rice in a pan, cover with water and mix thoroughly with a wooden spoon to break up any lumps. Bring to a boil, stirring occasionally, cover and simmer gently over a flame spreader for 20-30 minutes. Serve with the seeds and a small amount of umeboshi plum.

YANNOH COFFEE

1 dessertspoonful of Yannoh coffee per serving
Boiling water
Coffee filter

Filter the Yannoh just like ordinary coffee or bring water to a boil in a pan and simmer the coffee for a few minutes. When you boil Yannoh, it tends to foam over, so use a large pan and have some cold water handy to add if this happens. Strain and serve.

ALTERNATIVELY - you can get an instant variety of Yannoh which can be used just like any other instant coffee.

■ SNACKS

Bancha tea, rice cakes with peanut butter or sugar-free jam

■ LUNCH - USING LEFTOVERS

FOR WORK:- Carry leftovers (from supper) to work in a strong container. Preferrably acquire a glass, stainless steel or lacquer lunch box or a good quality, hard plastic one if nothing else. You can pack the box with your lunch at suppertime the night before or at breakfast time. Keep it cool but preferrably not in the refrigerator. Place the food attractively and each dish separately in the container so that it looks good as well as tasty - your workmates are bound to be curious and you want to impress them! Try not to take cauliflower - this always seems to smell rather strong and puts people off. You can keep a jar of condiment, like gomasio or some roasted seeds at work ready for use, plus some bancha tea bags or instant Yannoh. If you have some noodles left from the day before, you can take these or some rice with lentil stew and perhaps a freshly boiled vegetable prepared while making your breakfast. This will only take a couple of minutes.

AT HOME:- Steam some ready-cooked rice or noodles and serve with leftover lentil stew. Serve with toasted nori and seeds and one or two lightly steamed or boiled vegetables. You can steam the rice or noodles by placing in a bowl and putting this inside a pan with a little boiling water, tightly covered. Alternatively, place the rice or noodles into a stainless steel steamer. To toast the nori, hold a sheet over a naked flame and gently move about so that it does not burn. Toast until it is a lovely green colour all over. Cut into thin strips or little squares. Store any extra pieces in a jar for future use.

■ SNACKS

Bancha Tea and ready-prepared seeds, nuts and raisins

■ DINNER
MISO SOUP
FRIED RICE
LEFTOVER BEAN DISH
BOILED SALAD
BANCHA TEA OR YANNOH

MISO SOUP

2 leeks, washed and finely sliced on the diagonal
1 small parsnip, quartered and finely sliced
1 x 5 inch piece wakame, rinsed and soaked in a little cold water
2 level dessertspoons of mugi miso
Finely sliced spring onion for garnish
2 pints water

Bring water to the boil and add the leeks. Simmer for 5-10 minutes and then add the parsnip. Simmer for another 5 minutes and then add the finely sliced wakame and the soaking fluid. Simmer for a further 5 minutes, then turn the heat to very low so that there is just the most gentle simmer. Make a puree of the miso with some of the soup liquid and then add this to the soup. Simmer for 4-5 minutes and then serve garnished with the spring onion (cut on the diagonal, very finely, looks best).

FRIED RICE

2 cups ready cooked rice
2 onions finely sliced
2 carrots quartered and diced
Soy sauce
Ginger juice
Sesame oil
Roasted sesame seeds

The method for this dish is very much the same as for the rice and beans with vegetables on day 5 lunch. Proceed in the same way adding the carrot instead of the celery and garnishing with sesame seeds.

LEFTOVER BEAN DISH

If you have plain cooked beans or lentils, cook some vegetables in water until soft and then add the beans to heat through. Season with miso or soy sauce and some ginger juice if you wish and serve with some chopped parsley. If your beans are already prepared with vegetables, heat them through gently in a saucepan with a little extra water if necessary or place them in a covered dish in a medium oven to heat through.

DAY THREE

■ **BREAKFAST**

STEAMED BREAD WITH SESAME/TAHINI SPREAD
OR SUGAR-FREE JAM
BANCHA/YANNOH
OPTIONAL - LEFTOVER MISO SOUP

STEAMED BREAD

Steam slices of sourdough bread in a bamboo or stainless steel steamer just long enough to moisten and soften. Spread with tahini or jam or make a spread by sauté-ing some sliced onion in a little water until soft, then add miso to season, simmer another 3 minutes and then add some tahini. This can be stored in a jar in the fridge for 3-4 days.

MISO SOUP

When using leftover soup, heat through gently but do not boil. Garnish with freshly sliced spring onion or parsley.

■ **SNACKS**

Bancha tea or Yannoh. Rice cakes etc.

■ LUNCH

FOR WORK:- Use leftovers for work such as noodles or rice, or make up some sandwiches with sourdough bread - tahini with sauerkraut or some homemade spread as described above under breakfast.

AT HOME:- COUSCOUS AND BOILED SALAD

COUSCOUS

1 cup couscous
1 1/2 cups water
Pinch sea salt
3 spring onions
1-2 tsp miso
1 onion finely sliced
6 mushrooms

Rinse couscous in a wire sieve under the tap and leave to drain. Bring water to the boil and add the couscous and salt. Bring back to a boil, turn the heat to very low, cover and simmer for 5 minutes. Turn off the heat and let the pan stand for 20 minutes without removing the cover. When ready, transfer couscous to a bowl and fluff up with a fork. Meanwhile, sauté the onion in a little water until soft and then add the mushrooms, finely sliced. Cook until the mushrooms are soft and then add some miso made into a purée with a little cold water. Simmer gently for another 5 minutes, adding more water if necessary to make a sauce-like consistency and then pour over the couscous. Sprinkle the spring onions over the top and serve.

BOILED SALAD

1 cup broccoli florets
1 cup daikon cut lengthwise into quarters and then finely sliced
Rice vinegar
Umeboshi vinegar

Bring some water to a boil (about 1 pint) and add the daikon. Boil for 1-2 minutes and then remove from the pan and drain. Now boil the broccoli 1-2 minutes and drain also. Make up a dressing with the vinegars and a little of the cooking liquid to your taste. Pour dressing over the vegetables in a bowl and mix thoroughly.

■ SNACKS

Bancha or yannoh.
Sugar-free biscuits.

Check the ingredients' list on the biscuits and avoid those containing sugar or honey. Good shops will stock some sweetened with raisins, apple juice, rice syrup or barley malt. Keep them in an airtight tin and keep some at work for snacks.

■ DINNER

UDON NOODLES IN BROTH
PAN-FRIED TOFU
PRESSED SALAD (SEE DAY 6 - LUNCH)
PICKLE
STEWED APPLES WITH ALMONDS
BANCHA OR YANNOH

UDON NOODLES IN BROTH

1 packet udon wholewheat noodles cooked as described on Day 1
2 pints water
1 x 3 inch strip kombu
2 onions finely sliced
2-3 tbsps soy sauce
Finely sliced spring onion

Place the kombu into the cold water in a saucepan and bring to the boil. Simmer for 5 minutes and then remove the kombu which can be kept in a jar in the refrigerator and saved for further use. Add the sliced onions to the water and simmer until very soft before adding the soy sauce and simmering for a further 2-3 minutes. Pour over the hot noodles in individual bowls and garnish with the spring onion.

PAN FRIED TOFU WITH DIPPING SAUCE

1 pack regular tofu
Flour
Oil for frying
Soy sauce
Ginger juice

Wrap the tofu in absorbent kitchen paper for a few minutes to dry and then cut into thin slices. Dip the slices into flour to coat and heat the oil in a heavy frying pan. Fry the tofu slices until lightly golden and then drain on more paper. Make up a dip sauce by combining the soy sauce with the ginger juice. Serve sauce in a bowl so that the tofu can be dipped into it before eating.

PICKLE

You can buy good quality daikon pickle. It is called Tekkuan and comes in long pieces which you slice very thinly. You only need a small amount, perhaps 3 or 4 slices. Store the rest in a jar in the refrigerator.

STEWED APPLES WITH ALMONDS

1 pound eating apples, unpeeled but cored and finely sliced
Roasted almonds
Water
Pinch sea salt
2 tsps kuzu

When slicing the apples, place them in a bowl of salted water so that they do not go brown. Once they are all sliced, place in a saucepan with a little of the salted water and simmer until just soft. Dissolve the kuzu in a little cold water and stir into the apples making sure that they are not boiling fast, they should be just on a very low simmer. Stir until thickened and then serve hot or allow to cool, garnished with chopped, roasted almonds.

DAY FOUR

■ **BREAKFAST**
PORRIDGE OATS WITH ROASTED ALMONDS
BANCHA OR YANNOH

PORRIDGE OATS
Cook jumbo oats as described in day 1 and serve with some ready roasted almonds.

□ ***PREPARATION FOR THE EVENING MEAL***

Take one cup of azuki beans and sort through for stones and grit. Wash the beans thoroughly in a wire sieve under the cold tap and place them in a bowl. Cover with water, place a plate or cloth over the top and leave to soak until the evening.

■ **SNACKS**
Rice cakes with spreads as above

■ **LUNCH**

FOR WORK:- Use leftover noodles with a little of the broth from the night before if practical and maybe a couple of lightly boiled vegetables.

AT HOME:-
Corn On the cob with umeboshi or wholewheat pasta
Boiled vegetables with sauce

CORN ON THE COB

1 cob of whole fresh corn per serving
Umeboshi purée
Water
Sea salt

Bring plenty of water to the boil, add a pinch of sea salt and add the cobs of corn. Boil until soft, about 5-6 minutes and drain. Mix some umeboshi purée with a little of the cooking liquid and spread over the corn cobs before serving.

WHOLEWHEAT PASTA

Wholewheat pasta
Water
Pinch sea salt
Onion finely sliced
Kuzu
Soy sauce
Whole grain mustard
Finely chopped parsley
Oil

Bring plenty of water to the boil, add the sea salt and pasta and stir thoroughly. Check the manufacturer's instructions on the pasta packet for cooking times and amount required per portion. When cooked, drain and rinse under the cold tap to avoid sticking. Next, fry the onion in the heated oil until soft and translucent, add some water and the soy sauce to taste and simmer for a few minutes. Add some mustard and then thicken the mixture with a little kuzu dissolved in cold water. Stir in the noodles and heat through gently before serving garnished with the chopped parsley.

BOILED VEGETABLES WITH SAUCE

Carrots sliced in thin rounds
Cabbage sliced
Water
Pinch sea salt
Tahini

Bring water to the boil, add the sea salt and the carrots and boil for 1-2 minutes. Drain thoroughly. Now boil the cabbage and drain. Mix vegetables together in a bowl and stir in a sauce made from the tahini and some of the vegetable cooking liquid.

■ SNACKS

Bancha or Yannoh. Sugar-free biscuits or roasted seeds, nuts and raisins.

■ DINNER

MISO SOUP
RICE WITH AZUKI BEANS
GOMASIO
BOILED DAIKON WITH PARSLEY
BAKED PUMPKIN, CARROT & PARSNIPS
TOASTED NORI

It is best to prepare the rice and beans first, followed by the baked vegetables, then the soup finishing with the boiled daikon and toasted nori.

RICE WITH AZUKI BEANS

3 cups rice washed and drained as in Day 1
1 cup azuki beans soaked
1 x 4 inch strip kombu wiped
5 1/2 cups water

Place the kombu in the bottom of the pressure cooker. Mix the beans with the rice and place on top of the kombu. Add the water, pouring gently down the sides of the rice and beans (you can use the bean soaking water as part of the cooking water).Cover the cooker and bring to pressure. Cook for 50 minutes. Bring down the pressure and transfer the beans and rice to a bowl as described in day one. Serve sprinkled with gomasio which you can make at home or buy ready-made. If you do not have a pressure cooker, boil the beans on their own for 15 minutes first before adding to the rice with the required amount of water and boiling for 50 minutes.

GOMASIO

14-16 teaspoons sesame seeds, sorted, washed and drained
1 teaspoon sea salt

Heat a stainless steel or cast iron frying pan and add the sea salt. Stir around in the pan with a wooden spoon for a few minutes until shiny. Transfer the sea salt to a suribachi[1] and grind to a fine powder. Now place the sesame seeds in the pan making sure they are well-drained but still moist, otherwise they may burn if too dry. Stir the seeds gently with a wooden spoon and do not let the pan get too hot. Roast the seeds for about 5-10 minutes. They are ready when they smell quite nutty and you can easily crush them between your thumb and a finger. Quickly transfer to the suribachi with the salt and gently grind them in a circular motion with a wooden surikogi until half ground. Do not use too much pressure and don't rush. Let the gomasio cool completely before transferring to a jar to store. Gomasio will keep several weeks but it is better to get into the habit of making it weekly. This way your technique will improve more readily.

BAKED PUMPKIN, CARROTS AND PARSNIPS

Pumpkin, carrot and parsnips cut into large chunks
Water
Sea salt

Boil the parsnips for about 4-5 minutes and drain. Add with the other vegetables to a casserole dish and enough water to cover the base of the dish to about 1/4 inch. Sprinkle with a little sea salt, cover and place in a medium, pre-heated oven. Cook for about 45-60 minutes or until the vegetables are

1 A suribachi is an earthenware mortar with ridges inside which is very useful for purééing miso and crushing seeds. The wooden surikoge is used to do the grinding. These items are available in oriental and specialised food shops. If not available, try using a pestle and mortar.

soft. Baked vegetables are made richer by brushing with a little oil. Cover with foil in a baking tin if you do not have a covered dish.

MISO SOUP

You can make the soup the same way as on day 2 but substituting the vegetables as follows:- 2 onions, finely sliced and 2-3 carrots cut in half lengthwise and then thinly sliced.

BOILED DAIKON WITH PARSLEY

Daikon thinly sliced in rounds, half-rounds or quarter-rounds
Chopped parsley
Water
Pinch sea salt

Bring water to a fast boil, add salt and daikon and cook for 1-2 minutes. Drain and serve garnished with the parsley. You can make a dressing with soy sauce and rice vinegar.

TOASTED NORI

1 Sheet Nori

Hold sheet of nori flat over a medium flame and move about gently to toast it evenly.It should be a nice even green colour when done. Be careful not to let it burn. Snip into little squares or thin strips and store in a jar. Use to garnish soups, grains or vegetables dishes.

DAY FIVE

■ **BREAKFAST**

SOFT RICE WITH BEANS, ROASTED SEEDS & UMEBOSHI
OR
OAT PORRIDGE (AS BEFORE)
BANCHA OR YANNOH

SOFT RICE WITH BEANS

1 cup ready cooked rice with azuki beans
Water
1 umeboshi plum
Seeds

Place the rice and beans in a pan and cover with water. Cook slowly until soft and creamy, about 20-30 minutes on a flame spreader. Serve with the roasted seeds and umeboshi plum.

■ SNACKS

Rice cakes etc. as before

■ LUNCH

FOR WORK:- RICE BALLS

Cooked rice (or rice with beans)
Nori, toasted and quartered
Umeboshi plum

Take a medium handful of cooked rice in moistened hands and mould into a rough ball. Poke a hole to the centre and insert a quarter of an umeboshi plum. Fill in the hole and then start to apply even pressure around the edges of the rice with each hand alternately. Keep pressing for about 30 times until the rice is really firm and in the shape of a smooth round ball or a slightly triangular shape. Moisten hands again and then take one quarter of nori, shiny side out and place this in your palm. Put the rice ball in the middle and with your other hand start to gently mould the nori around the sides of the ball. Keep doing this until the moisture on your hands and in the rice ball has adhered the nori to the rice. Now take another piece of nori in your palm and invert the rice ball onto it so that you can mould this piece around until the ball is completely covered with nori. Do not get your hands too wet as this will make the nori too soggy. You can repair any holes with tiny pieces of moistened nori. Rice balls travel well wrapped in sushi mats with a rubber band around and then placed in a paper bag.

AT HOME:-

LEFTOVER RICE AND BEANS WITH FRIED ONION & CELERY, STEAMED CHINESE LEAF WITH SAUERKRAUT

RICE AND BEANS WITH VEGETABLES

1 onion sliced
2 stalks celery sliced
1 cup leftover rice and beans
Sesame oil
Soy sauce
Ginger juice (optional)
Water
Sliced spring onion

Fry the onion in a little oil for about 5 minutes, stirring continually. Add the celery and fry for another two minutes. Add water to cover vegetables and place the rice and beans on top. Cover and simmer until the vegetables are soft. Season with some soy sauce and the ginger juice, if used. Simmer for 2-3 minutes and serve garnished with the spring onion.

STEAMED CHINESE LEAF WITH SAUERKRAUT

Chinese leaves finely sliced
Water
Pinch sea salt
Sauerkraut

Place the leaves in a steamer and cook over hot water for about 1-2 minutes. Remove and place in a bowl. Mix in some drained sauerkraut and serve.

■ SNACKS

Bancha tea or Yannoh. Sugar-free biscuits or toasted seeds, nuts and raisins.

■ DINNER

LEFTOVER MISO SOUP
STEAMED RICE AND BEANS
BOILED SALAD
HIZIKI WITH ONION
SWEET VEGETABLE STEW
SAUERKRAUT

STEAMED RICE AND BEANS

Put rice and beans in a bowl and place in a pan with about one inch of boiling water in the bottom. Cover and simmer until heated through. Serve with some toasted seeds.

BOILED SALAD

Using the method described before, boil a selection of vegetables and serve with a dressing of water, rice vinegar and umeboshi vinegar, soy sauce, mustard and water, mirin (sweet rice wine) and soy sauce, ginger juice and soy sauce. You can use most vegetables including carrots, onions, leeks, parsnips, daikon, red radish, celery, chinese leaf, swede, turnip, cucumber, broccoli, cauliflower etc.

HIZIKI WITH ONIONS

1 small cup hiziki
Toasted sesame oil
2 onions, sliced
2 tbsps soy sauce
Water

Place the hiziki on a plate to shake off the dust and then place it in a bowl of water to cover. Swish around with your fingers to rinse it and then discard the water. Do this about 3 times in all then drain. Sauté the onions in the hot oil for a few minutes and then place the hiziki on top. Cover the onions with water and bring to the boil. Reduce heat and simmer, covered, for about 40 minutes. Add the soy sauce and simmer uncovered until all the liquid has gone.

SWEET VEGETABLE STEW

2 Onions cut into eighths
1/4 Medium pumpkin cut into chunks about 1" square
3 Carrots cut into 1" chunks
1/4 Medium white cabbage cut into chunks
Water
Sea salt

Place the onions into a pan and cover with the pumpkin and then the carrots. Add water to cover the onions, sprinkle with a little sea salt, cover and bring to a boil. Cook for about 10 minutes and then add the cabbage on top. Add a little more water if necessary, cover and continue simmering until all the vegetables are soft. Check that steam is coming out of the side of the pan - if not, the liquid has dried up and needs replenishing quickly! Serve piping hot.

DAY SIX

■ **BREAKFAST**
STEAMED SOURDOUGH BREAD WITH SPREADS (TAHINI, HOMEMADE ONION / MISO / TAHINI SPREAD AS ABOVE OR SUGAR-FREE JAM)
BANCHA OR YANNOH

□ ***PREPARATION FOR EVENING COOKING***

WHOLE OAT PORRIDGE

Wash as you would for rice, drain and cover with water to the proportion of 1 cup whole oats to 5 cups water. Cover and leave to soak until the evening.

■ **SNACKS** - AS BEFORE

■ LUNCH

FOR WORK:- Use leftovers (see above for ideas)

AT HOME:-
MILLET WITH ONION AND CAULIFLOWER, GRAVY, PRESSED SALAD

MILLET WITH ONION AND CAULIFLOWER

1 cup millet
1 onion, diced
About 1 1/2 cups cauliflower florets
1/4 teaspoon sea salt
3 1/2 cups water

Place millet in a wire sieve and place under cold water tap to wash. Drain thoroughly and then dry roast in a cast iron or stainless steel frying pan. Stir continually for about 5 minutes ensuring that millet does not burn. There should be a nutty aroma when done. Place the water to boil while you are doing this and then add the roasted millet, onion, cauliflower and sea salt. Bring to the boil, cover and simmer gently for about 30 minutes. Transfer to a bowl and mash with a fork.

GRAVY

1 onion, diced
6 mushrooms, chopped
1/2 pint water
Soy sauce
Chopped parsley
Kuzu

Place the vegetables in a pan and cover with the water. Bring to a boil and simmer until the vegetables are soft. Season with the soy sauce and simmer for 2 minutes. Thicken slightly with a little kuzu dissolved in cold water. Stir in the parsley and use to pour over the millet.

PRESSED SALAD

Half a cucumber, thinly sliced
About 12 red radishes, thinly sliced
Sea salt
Rice vinegar

Place the vegetables in a pickle press and sprinkle with some sea salt. Mix thoroughly. If you do not have a pickle press, place the vegetables in a shallow bowl with the salt, mix and cover with a plate and put a weight on top (a brick or a pot of water will do). Press for 1 - 2 hours then drain thoroughly. If too salty, you can rinse with water and if you wish you can finish pressing by squeezing with your hands. Add some rice vinegar to taste, or some lemon juice.

ALTERNATIVES:- finely cut chinese leaf or cabbage, grated or thinly sliced carrot, celery, daikon.

■ **SNACKS** - as before

■ **DINNER**

UDON NOODLES WITH BROTH
DEEP FRIED TEMPEH WITH LEMON AND GRATED DAIKON
STEAMED GREENS WITH SAUERKRAUT

COOK WHOLE OATS FOR NEXT DAY'S BREAKFAST

UDON NOODLES WITH BROTH - Proceed as before

DEEP-FRIED TEMPEH WITH LEMON AND GRATED DAIKON

1 block tempeh, thoroughly thawed (you can leave it out in the morning to thaw)
Lemon wedges
Grated daikon
Soy sauce
Oil for deep-frying

Heat oil and fry the tempeh in small cubes until a rich golden brown colour. When you place the tempeh into the hot oil it should sink and then quickly rise to the top. If it stays on the bottom, then the oil is not hot enough. When cooked, drain the tempeh on some absorbent kitchen paper. Serve with the lemon and a small bowl of grated daikon with a few drops of soy sauce on it.

STEAMED GREENS - Proceed as before and mix with sauerkraut.

WHOLE OAT PORRIDGE

Place the already soaked oats and water in a large saucepan, adding 1 pinch of sea salt per cup of oats. Bring to a boil, stir thoroughly, cover, reduce flame to very low and place a flame spreader over it. Cook for several hours, very slowly, giving it an occasional stir. The oats should be very creamy and soft when done.

ALTERNATIVELY:- Cook the oats in a pressure cooker - bring to a boil uncovered and simmer for about 10 minutes. Skim off any husks (these may block the valve if left), cover and bring to pressure. Reduce flame to low and cover with a flame spreader. Cook for about 50 minutes.

DAY SEVEN

■ **BREAKFAST**

WHOLE OAT PORRIDGE WITH UMEBOSHI,
BARLEY MALT OR SEEDS
BANCHA TEA

PORRIDGE OATS

Cooked oats
Water
Umeboshi plum, barley malt or toasted seeds

If you cooked your oats the night before as described, place enough for you needs in a saucepan and add a little water. Break up the oats with a wooden spoon so that there are no lumps and then heat through gently until hot.

□ *PREPARATION FOR THE EVENING MEAL*

Wash some barley as in the rice method and soak with 1 1/2 cups of water per cup of grain. Leave covered until the evening.

■ SNACKS

Bancha tea or Yannoh, rice cakes with peanut butter or sugar-free jam.

■ LUNCH

SMOKED TOFU SANDWICHES
RAW VEGETABLES

SMOKED TOFU SANDWICHES

Sourdough bread sliced and steamed
Smoked tofu, sliced
Tahini
Sauerkraut

Spread the bread thinly with tahini and arrange tofu and sauerkraut in sandwich form and cover with more tahini spread bread.

RAW VEGETABLES

A selection of vegetables
Dressing

Select some fresh vegetables, carrots, cucumber, celery, cabbage and wash thoroughly. Cut carrots, cucumber or celery into sticks and finely shred cabbage. Serve with a dressing made of umeboshi purée and a little water, or some soy sauce with grain mustard

■ **SNACKS**

Bancha or yannoh

Sugar-free biscuits or roasted seeds, nuts and raisins

■ **DINNER**

MISO SOUP WITH BARLEY, PUMPKIN, CARROTS AND PARSNIPS
STEAMED WHITE FISH
COUSCOUS WITH MISO AND VEGETABLE SAUCE
STEAMED GREENS
BOILED SALAD
DAIKON PICKLES

MISO SOUP WITH BARLEY

1 cup cooked barley (see below)
2 onions, sliced
1 carrot, sliced into rounds
About 1 cup of pumpkin cut into small cubes
1 small parsnip, quartered lengthwise and thinly sliced
2 level dessertspoonsful of mugi miso
Spring onion, finely sliced for garnish
2 pints cold water

Pressure cook or boil the barley as for brown rice in the ratio of 1 cup barley to 1½ cups water and 1 pinch sea salt. While this is cooking, prepare the vegetables for the soup. Place the onions in the bottom of a large saucepan and cover with the pumpkin, parsnips, carrots and the cooked barley. Add the water, bring to the boil and simmer covered until the vegetables are soft. Purée the miso with a small amount of the soup liquid, turn down the flame to a very low simmer and then add the purée. Simmer gently for a few minutes and serve with the spring onion garnish.

STEAMED WHITE FISH

Cod or plaice fillets (1 per person)
Soy sauce
Brown rice vinegar
Lemon slices

Wash the fish in salted water and pat dry. Place in a stainless steel steamer and steam until cooked through. Alternatively, place in a pan with a little water and steam, covered until done. Serve with a dressing of soy sauce and rice vinegar and a garnish of lemon slices. A little parsley adds a nice touch as well.

COUSCOUS WITH MISO AND VEGETABLE SAUCE

Prepare as in the recipe on day three. Vary the vegetables if you wish by omitting mushrooms and adding small carrot dice.

STEAMED GREENS

Kale, spring greens, brussel tops, broccoli etc.

Steam as on day one.

BOILED SALAD

Follow the method as before but vary the vegetables as much as possible and change your salad dressings.

DAY EIGHT

■ BREAKFAST

WHOLE OAT PORRIDGE WITH UMEBOSHI, BARLEY MALT OR ROASTED SEEDS OR NUTS

BANCHA OR YANNOH

WHOLE OAT PORRIDGE

Re-heat ready cooked whole oat porridge as described on day seven and serve with a condiment of your choice as listed above.

□ *PREPARATION FOR THE EVENING MEAL*

BARLEY

Soak some barley as described on day seven.

CHICKPEAS

Sort the chickpeas for stones or grit and wash thoroughly in a wire sieve under a cold tap. Place in a large bowl and cover with cold water (3 cups water to 1 cup of chickpeas). Cover bowl and leave to stand 6-8 hours.

■ SNACKS

Bancha or Yannoh. Rice cakes with peanut butter or sugar-free jam.

■ LUNCH

FOR WORK:- Take leftover couscous and sauce and some steamed tofu. You can steam the tofu in a stainless steel steamer or in a saucepan with a little water for about 5 minutes.

AT HOME:-
PAN-FRIED MOCHI WITH DAIKON AND SOY SAUCE
BOILED SALAD
SAUERKRAUT

PAN-FRIED MOCHI

Dried mochi (pounded sweet rice cakes)
Grated daikon
Soy sauce
Oil

Heat a little oil in a frying pan and fry the mochi on both sides for a few minutes until puffed up and lightly browned. Drain on absorbent paper and serve with grated daikon with a few drops of soy sauce on it.

BOILED SALAD

prepared as before.

■ SNACKS

Bancha or Yannoh.
Sugar-free biscuits or roasted seeds, nuts and raisins.

■ **DINNER**
MISO SOUP
RICE WITH BARLEY AND GOMASIO
CHICKPEA STEW
ARAME WITH BOILED SALAD
PRESSED SALAD
TOASTED NORI

START WITH CHICKPEAS THEN THE GRAIN FOLLOWED BY THE VEGETABLE DISHES.

COOKING CHICKPEAS

1 cup chickpeas, soaked
1 x 3 inch piece of kombu
Soaking water from the chickpeas
¼ to ½ teaspoon sea salt

Chickpeas are a versatile pulse, particularly useful when entertaining. Long soaking and cooking are important to get the best results but you can cook enough to transform into several different dishes over a few days - in soups, stews, salads and hummus - just cool any leftover, cooked chickpeas and store in a sealed jar in the refrigerator until needed. Soaking the chickpeas makes them easier to cook and more digestible.

TO COOK:- wipe the kombu and place in the bottom of a large, heavy-based saucepan. Place the chickpeas on top with the soaking liquid and bring to a boil. Boil for about 10 minutes uncovered and remove any scum that forms before covering with a lid to continue the cooking. Cook until quite soft, usually about one hour, adding more cold water if necessary. When soft, add the sea salt and continue cooking until almost all of the liquid has gone. Never add the salt before the beans have softened. If you add it too soon, the beans may not soften at all. If you wish to pressure cook the chickpeas, they will take 45-60 minutes. Use in recipes as follows:-

CHICKPEA STEW

1 cup cooked chickpeas
1 large carrot, diced
1 onion, diced
Soy sauce
Ginger juice
Kuzu
Parsley
Oil

Sauté the onion in the hot oil until soft and then add the carrot. Sauté for a couple of minutes and then add the chickpeas, any cooking liquid and, if necessary, some cold water to give a stew consistency. Simmer, covered, until the vegetables are soft and then add a small amount of shoyu and some ginger juice to taste. Continue simmering for a further 3-4 minutes and then thicken with a little kuzu, dissolved in cold water. Serve garnished with chopped parsley.

HUMMUS

2 cups cooked chickpeas
1 clove garlic
1 dessertspoonful umeboshi paste
1 dessertspoonful grain mustard
1-2 dessertspoonful tahini
1-2 dessertspoonful lemon juice

Blend the ingredients together, add a little cold water or cooking liquid if needed. Serve on steamed bread, rice cakes or stuffed into steamed wholemeal pitta bread with some green salad, pickled gherkins, lemon wedges and parsley. Hummus will keep for a few days in a sealed container in the refrigerator.

CHICKPEA SALAD

Mix cooked chickpeas with a selection of contrasting coloured vegetables - small cut and lightly boiled (still nice and crunchy) and add some raw, chopped spring onions and a few good quality black olives. Make a tasty dressing such as tahini, mustard, soy sauce and chickpea cooking liquid or a little water and rice vinegar or lemon juice.

RICE WITH BARLEY

1 cup soaked barley and the soaking liquid
1 cup rice, washed and drained
Extra 1 1/2 cups water
2 pinches sea salt

Place all ingredients together in a large pot or pressure cooker and cook for 45-50 minutes. Follow procedure as on day two.

ARAME WITH BOILED SALAD

Broccoli florets
Red radishes
1 cup arame
Water
Soy sauce
Brown rice vinegar

Place the arame in a bowl and cover with water. Swish around to remove dust and drain. Do this twice more and on the final rinse, save the water for cooking. Place the arame in a saucepan and half cover with the water taking care not to pour any dust in. Bring to a boil and simmer covered for 15-20 minutes and then drain. You can season with a little soy sauce if you wish or alternatively season the salad as a whole when complete. Boil the vegetables as previously described, drain and mix in a bowl with the cooked arame. Make a dressing with soy sauce, rice vinegar and some of the cooking liquid from the arame or some cold water. Mix well.

PREPARE PRESSED SALAD AND TOASTED NORI AS PREVIOUSLY DESCRIBED.

DAY NINE

■ BREAKFAST

SOFT RICE AND BARLEY WITH MISO
BANCHA OR YANNOH

SOFT RICE AND BARLEY WITH MISO

1 cup cooked grain
1/4 cup cooked beans or chickpeas
1/2 onion, sliced
1 carrot, diced
2 teaspoons miso
Water
Sliced spring onion

Place the onion in the bottom of a saucepan and cover with the carrots, beans and cooked grain. Add enough water to cover the vegetables and beans, cover pan and simmer for about 20 minutes. Add the miso, puréed with a little cold water and simmer gently for 2-3 minutes. Serve garnished with the spring onion.

■ SNACKS

Bancha or Yannoh.
Rice cakes with peanut butter or sugar-free jam.

■ LUNCH

FOR WORK:- Take some grain and chickpea stew or make up sandwiches or pittas with hummus as described on day eight.

AT HOME:-

CARROT SOUP
GRAIN AND VEGETABLE CROQUETTES
RAW SALAD

CARROT SOUP

4 sliced carrots
2 onions, diced
2 pints water
1/4 teaspoon sea salt
Fine strips of toasted nori for garnish

Place the onions and carrots in a pot with cold water and a pinch of sea salt. Bring to a boil. Simmer covered on a low heat for about 20 minutes. Add the rest of the salt and simmer for another 5-10 minutes. Serve garnished with the nori strips.

GRAIN CROQUETTES

2 cups ready-cooked grain
1 onion, diced
2 carrots, grated
Water
Wholewheat flour
Oil for frying

Mix the grain with the vegetables in a bowl, add some flour and a little water to bind and then shape into croquettes. Roll croquettes in a little flour and fry in hot oil until golden brown on all sides and beginning to get crisp. You can deep-fry them if you wish. When cooked, drain on absorbent kitchen paper. Any cooked grain can be used like this.

RAW SALAD

Lettuce washed and drained
Cucumber, halved lengthwise and finely sliced
Red radishes, grated
Umeboshi vinegar
Brown rice vinegar
Water

Mix the vegetables together and toss with a dressing made from the vinegars and a little water.

DINNER

CHICKPEA SOUP
FRIED RICE WITH CARROTS, ONIONS, CELERY AND SESAME SEEDS
STEAMED GREENS
VEGETABLE STEW WITH DEEP-FRIED TOFU AND KOMBU
PICKLES

Start with the vegetable stew, followed by the rice, then the soup and finally the greens.

VEGETABLE STEW WITH DEEP-FRIED TOFU AND KOMBU

1 leek, finely sliced
3 carrots, in chunks
2 small parsnips, in chunks
1 x 3 inch piece kombu, wiped, soaked and thinly sliced
1 block regular tofu
Miso
Oil for deep frying
Water
Chopped parsley for garnish
Kuzu
Flour

Place kombu in the base of a heavy saucepan and cover with the leek, parsnips and carrots. Cover the vegetables with water, bring to the boil, cover pan and simmer. Meanwhile, dry the tofu in some absorbent paper and cut into squares.Dip in some flour and deep fry until golden. Remove and drain. Add the tofu to the stew and continue simmering until the vegetables are soft. Turn heat to very low and take a little of the cooking liquid to make a purée with the miso. Add this to the pot and simmer for a couple of minutes. You can thicken the liquid with a little kuzu dissolved in cold water. Place in a serving bowl and garnish with the parsley. For extra taste, you can add some ginger juice at the end of cooking. For extra richness you can sauté the leeks in a little oil before adding the other vegetables, or you can place the stew in a covered dish in a medium oven for 20 minutes at the end of cooking.

FRIED RICE WITH CARROTS, ONIONS, CELERY AND SESAME SEEDS

You can follow the recipe on day five for this dish but add some sliced or matchstick carrots with the vegetables. If you use ginger juice in the stew then you can use mirin in this dish instead or just the soy sauce.

CHICKPEA SOUP

1 cup cooked chickpeas
2 onions, sliced
1 cup cauliflower florets
Sea salt
Watercress for garnish
2 pints water

Place the onions in a saucepan and add the water and a pinch of sea salt. Bring to the boil and simmer about 20 minutes. Add the cauliflower and chickpeas and simmer for 3-4 minutes. Then add a little more salt to taste, and simmer for 2 minutes. Serve garnished with sprigs of watercress.

STEAMED GREENS

Follow method as described before.

DAY TEN

■ **BREAKFAST**

JUMBO PORRIDGE OATS WITH SEEDS AND BARLEY MALT
BANCHA OR YANNOH

Make the oats as previously described and serve with seeds and/or barley malt.

☐ *PREPARATION FOR THE EVENING MEAL*

Wash and soak some whole barley as previously described using 1 cup of grain to 1 1/2 cups water.

■ SNACKS

Bancha or Yannoh. Rice cakes with peanut butter or sugar-free jam.

■ LUNCH

FOR WORK:- Take leftover rice with stew from the night before plus a little boiled green dish prepared at breakfast time.

AT HOME:- SUSHI

SUSHI

For each sushi you will need:-

1 sheet toasted nori
About 1 cup cooked rice
1 strip of carrot and 1 strip of cucumber the same length as the nori sheet
Tahini and sauerkraut, or mustard and umeboshi purée

Place the nori on a sushi mat. Take the rice and with moistened hands press it gently and evenly over the nori, leaving between 1/2 and 1 inch space at the end furthest from you (top) and a space of about a quarter of an inch on the end nearest to you (bottom). Boil the carrot strip for 4-5 minutes, drain and cool, then place this lengthwise about 1 inch in from the bottom end of the rice. Place the cucumber strip next to the carrot and then take your chosen flavourings as follows:- tahini and sauerkraut - spread the tahini along the vegetables with a spoon and then top with some drained sauerkraut. Mustard and umeboshi purée - spread both of these along the vegetables with a teaspoon. Start to roll up the sushi from the bottom making sure that the vegetables stay in place. Add firm pressure as you continue rolling and remember to pull the end of the sushi mat out as you go along. When completely rolled, moisten the end of the nori and press to seal along the length. Take a very sharp knife and moisten it. Slice the sushi into about 6 - 8 pieces with a saw-like motion, wetting the knife between each slice. If you use a dry knife, the nori will tear.

■ SNACKS

Bancha or Yannoh. Sugar-free biscuits or roasted seeds, nuts and raisins.

■ DINNER

BARLEY STEW
BOILED SALAD
TEMPURA
STEAMED GREENS WITH DULSE

BARLEY STEW

2 cups soaked barley, plus the soaking water
2 additional cups of water
2 cups pumpkin cut into chunks (unskinned)
2 onions, diced
1 bay leaf
2 carrots, diced
Soy sauce
Ginger juice

Place the onion in a pressure cooker and layer the pumpkin followed by the bay leaf and carrot on top. Add the barley and all the water, cover and pressure cook for about 45 minutes. (If not using a pressure cooker, boil in a covered saucepan for 50-60 minutes). Bring down the pressure, uncover and season with the soy sauce and ginger juice. Simmer gently for about 5 minutes and serve.

TEMPURA

Carrot, thinly sliced
Onion cut into rings
Cauliflower florets
Parsley sprigs
1 cup wholewheat flour
1 cup water
Pinch sea salt
1 tablespoon of kuzu or arrowroot
Oil for deep frying
Grated daikon
Soy sauce
Ginger juice

Chill the water in the refrigerator and then prepare the vegetables. Whisk a batter with the water, flour, salt and kuzu or arrowroot and leave to stand for a few minutes. Heat the oil in a heavy pan. It should be about 2 inches deep. The oil is ready when a small piece of food is added and drops to the bottom and then quickly rises to the top. If the food stays on the bottom, the oil is too cool. If the food stays on the top, the oil is too hot. Do not let the oil smoke at all. Start dipping the vegetables into the batter and fry about 5-6 pieces at a time. They will take from 1 - 3 minutes usually and should be crisp and golden when done except the parsley which only takes a few seconds. Turn the vegetables once during cooking. Drain the cooked vegetables on some absorbent paper and keep them hot on a baking tray in a cool oven if you wish. Serve with some grated daikon and a dip sauce made from soy sauce and ginger juice. Pumpkin, thinly sliced, is also nice in tempura as well as broccoli. Matchsticks of carrot cooked in clusters, perhaps 6 -8 pieces are also very good as they stick together in groups. Skim the oil from time to time while cooking to remove any pieces of batter. For a lighter batter, use carbonated water.

STEAMED GREENS WITH DULSE

Green leaves
Dulse
Water

Steam the greens as previously described and cool. Take a small amount of dulse and check it thoroughly for stones or tiny shells. Place it in a bowl with water to cover and soak for about 5 minutes. Slice the dulse finely and mix with the greens.

Chapter 11

CRAVINGS

by Simon Brown

It is common for people beginning a macrobiotic diet to find it difficult not to eat certain foods. In my experience, people find sugar, dairy food and coffee most difficult to give up, whereas people are often amazed at how easy it is not to eat meat. After the first six weeks the body adjusts to the new tastes and, as time goes by, feels satisfied on a more healthy diet. However, even after several weeks, it is quite possible to experience strong cravings for foods you would prefer not to eat. I put these cravings into two categories, the first being what I call a nutritional craving and the other emotional cravings. A nutritional craving is when the body perceives it is lacking a certain element of nutrition and gives you a craving. The most obvious example would be craving liquid after something dry and salty. These cravings are important and need to be addressed. This is achieved by understanding what qualities the food you crave has and if it is a food you do not wish to eat, find similar qualities within your macrobiotic diet. For example, cheese is high in fat, salt, and calcium, is protein-rich and fermented. Foods that would share those qualities are tofu or tempeh, particularly if they are deep fried or in the case of tofu, baked with miso spread over it. They are high in calcium, protein-rich and fermented. In addition they can be made more oily by frying and more salty by adding shoyu, miso or sea salt. A craving for cheese also suggests that the overall diet needs to be richer and may require fried food or fish.

In the same way milk is high in fat, has calcium and is protein-rich. Tahini, a spread made from sesame seeds is also oily, contains calcium and is protein rich. Tahini can be used to make creamy sauces and desserts. Using these principles, I have listed a number of foods that may be craved and made suggestions of typical macrobiotic foods which provide a similar quality of nutrition.

NUTRITIONAL CRAVINGS

SUGAR

Try barley malt (malt extract), brown rice syrup or amazake. In addition, a craving for sweets can be caused by an excess of dry foods, salty foods or overcooked foods. Try reducing salty foods, increase lightly cooked vegetables, increase the use of sweet vegetables like carrots, parsnips, cabbage, pumpkin, onions or swedes. Finally chewing well and mixing each mouthful of food with saliva to begin the process of breaking down the cooked complex sugars (carbohydrates, starches or polysaccharides).

CHOCOLATE

Apart from the sweetness, chocolate has a roasted bitter quality. This is similar to roasted seeds or nuts. They can be sweetened by adding raisins.

REFINED FLOUR FOODS

These are typically commercial breads, biscuits or pastries. Instead, a good quality bread is recommended. These are known as natural rise, sourdough or yeast-free bread. Check the ingredients for added sugar or honey. This bread may be steamed to make it lighter and even more digestible. Other recommended flour products are noodles, whole wheat pasta and/or a wheat gluten product called seitan. It is now possible to find a good selection of biscuits made without sugar and sweetened with barley malt.

CHEESE

Try deep fried tofu, tempeh or mochi adding shoyu to taste. Increase fried dishes such as fried vegetables, fried rice and fried noodles. Use a small amount of cold pressed sesame, sunflower or corn oil. Also try using more fish including some oily fish.

MILK

An obvious substitute would be soya milk. However, as soya milk has relatively high concentrates of aluminium and is highly processed, soya milk tends to be used only occasionally for sauces. More often make creams using oats or tahini.

MEAT

For many people, the easiest substitute is fish. Although similar in terms of nutrition, fish is much lower in saturated fats than meat. Other options are to make croquettes (fried bean, grain and vegetable burgers) or to use a meat substitute called seitan, often known as wheat meat.

I have also known people who miss a more crunchy texture. To them, the macrobiotic diet seems consistently too soft. This texture can be achieved by adding roasted seeds or roasted chopped nuts to the food once it is cooked. I often sprinkle roasted seeds over my grains. A crispy taste can be created by deep-frying vegetables in a light batter. This special Japanese dish is called tempura.

If the food still tastes bland after the first six weeks, there are many ways of increasing the taste. Grated fresh root ginger will add a spicy taste, brown rice vinegar or umeboshi vinegar provide a sour taste, umeboshi plums a salty sour taste, barley malt or fruit juice a sweet taste, roasted nuts or seeds a bitter taste and sea salt, shoyu or miso different salty tastes. A common mistake is to only use the salty seasonings to increase taste. This often produces strong cravings for sweets. Far better is to incorporate all the available seasonings into your cooking. The Chinese have five different tastes to provide a healthy variety at meals. These are sweet, spicy, salty, sour and bitter. All these tastes are available to anyone eating macrobiotically.

EMOTIONAL CRAVINGS

Emotional cravings are those where particular foods are connected with an emotional feeling. For example, a child who is given chocolate when he behaves well but denied it when he behaves badly will inevitably feel better emotionally when eating chocolate. To him, chocolate will seem to be a reward for being good. We all have these connections in our past between food and emotional feelings. They are recognisable as cravings that occur when feeling a certain way or as something is drunk or eaten out of habit. A cup of coffee or a biscuit at 11am is a good example. The most positive approach is to use these natural connections to support a more healthy way of eating. This means that any time healthy foods are eaten, the situation needs to be as pleasurable as possible. So not only do the foods taste good, they look attractive, smell appetising, the table is beautifully set, you are listening to your favourite music and you eat with someone whose company you enjoy or perhaps reading an enjoyable book. As time goes by, positive associations will be created with healthy foods and once these associations become stronger than your past associations, you will feel better emotionally eating macrobiotic foods, than chocolate or whatever previously made you feel good.

Finally, some people find that on starting to eat macrobiotically, they eat much larger quantities. With a macrobiotic diet, people eat as much as they like. However I would recommend eating up to 90% capacity and wait for 30 minutes. If you still do not feel satisfied, make sure you are chewing well and that you are getting enough variety of cooking styles and ingredients. Most people have 3 meals a day, but it is fine to only eat twice a day. Whatever makes you feel good.

Chapter 12

NATURAL HEALTH CARE SUGGESTIONS

by Simon Brown

Although food is considered the foundation of good health there are many other influences on health that are important and contribute to the beneficial effect of the food. This chapter looks at ways to achieve this.

EATING

The ability to digest and absorb food is greatly enhanced by proper chewing. This is particularly important when chewing foods which contain cooked starches (complex sugars) like grain, vegetables or beans, as saliva contains an enzyme known as ptyalin which starts the process of breaking down these complex sugars into more simple sugars. Try chewing a mouthful of brown rice one hundred times and see if you notice the rice becoming sweeter as you chew. In addition, chewing well physically breaks down the food, massages the salivary glands and encourages a slower pace of eating. Eating too quickly can often cause indigestion. I would recommend always chewing more than 30 times a mouthful and ,when eating alone , at least 50 times. If I do not feel well I would then try to chew 100 times each mouthful until the food is completely liquid. As Ghandi said "Drink your food and chew your drink".

I always notice the benefit of eating when I am relaxed. Many people under stress become tense in their abdomen and secrete more acid into their digestive system. The digestive system is in constant motion during digestion, milling, mixing and moving the foods, through the actions of segmentation, tone waves and peristalsis. This movement will happen more easily when the surrounding muscles are relaxed.

Obviously gravity plays a part in the digestive system. Food starts near the top and slowly moves down to the bowel. In macrobiotics, it is therefore considered important not to lie down too soon after a meal. Food takes about four hours to reach the end of the small intestine after being eaten. So ideally, if someone usually goes to sleep at 11pm, they would eat by 7pm. This not only helps the food move smoothly through the digestive system but also ensures that much of the digestive work have been done before going to sleep. Once a meal has been eaten, a considerable amount of blood concentrates in the abdomen during the process of digestion. To go to sleep having recently eaten results in not only the process of digestion being slowed but also that less blood is available to repair and rebuild the body's cells during sleep. I always feel more energetic in the morning having gone to bed with a relatively empty stomach.

Another useful tip is to always sit down to eat. Sitting down creates a more physically relaxed environment for the stomach, whereas standing or walking stretches the stomach. However once the meal is finished, walking actually massages the lower intestine and helps the movement of food. So some relaxed activity or a walk is recommended shortly after a meal. When eating, the order in which the meal is eaten and how the foods are combined will also effect the process of digestion. The time taken to digest foods varies. For example, fruits are generally digested more quickly than grains. They would therefore make a poor combination if eaten together. A typical macrobiotic meal begins with soup seasoned with sea-salt, miso or shoyu and the main meal made up of grains, vegetables and beans or fish. The dessert, particularly if it contains fruit, would be then saved until an hour later. This gives the previous food a head start and allows the fruit to be digested at a quicker rate. Mixing fruit with grains or beans increases the likelihood of bloating, gas, or digestive discomfort.

DRINKING

It has become common for people to drink far more liquid than they normally feel they need. Many people advise drinking 8 glasses of water to flush the kidneys out. In addition, people often drink at meals, at work breaks, out of habit as well as the social ritual of drinking when meeting people. If someone was to listen to their body and only drink when they felt thirsty, they would find that they need much less liquid. Drinking too much liquid consistently can be eventually just as harmful as drinking too little.

All the excess liquid has to be absorbed into the blood. The liquid then dilutes the blood and also increases the strain on the heart as it has to pump this extra fluid. Finally the kidneys have to work harder to take the liquid back out of the blood. The symptoms of excess fluid are many. In my experience I have found that a significant number of people cannot sleep through the night without having to get up to urinate. This often improves if they just drink when thirsty. Many of these people also have lower back pain which again often gets better when they drink a natural amount of liquid. So it is recommended that people drink only when they are thirsty. After all, your own body is most likely to know when you need liquid. Of course there are exceptions to this. For example when you have a urinary infection, kidney stones or when you are not used to a hot climate. Apart from the quantity of liquid, I would also suggest not having iced cold liquids in a typical British climate, as this causes an unnecessary shock to the digestive system. Many people eating macrobiotically prefer not to drink at meals to avoid diluting their digestive juices.

UTENSILS

So as not to spoil the effect of all the healthy ingredients, it is necessary to avoid the use of 'soft' cooking utensils. These are primarily pots and pans make from aluminium or non-stick materials. A common cause for concern is that small amounts of aluminium oxide or toxic non-stick. materials will get into the food. Unfortunately both of these are considered harmful to the human body. Aluminium is currently implicated as a cause of Alzheimer's Disease. A simple experiment to try at home is to take an aluminium pot, add water until 1cm deep, and thoroughly scrub the bottom with a normal scotchbrite pan cleaner. After 2 minutes, squeeze out the pan cleaner and look at the water. If it has turned grey, you are seeing aluminium oxide that has been scraped off the surface of the pot. The most common hard-wearing materials used for macrobiotic cooking are stainless steel, enamel, Pyrex (oven-proof glass) and cast iron.

COOKERS

To benefit from the greatest amount of control during cooking, macrobiotic cooks recommend gas cookers rather than electric. The time-lag between setting the control and the electric heating element reaching the set temperature makes cooking on an electric cooker frustrating. In addition there has been significant information published in the U.S.A.[1] on the harmful effects of electromagnetic radiation from electrical appliances such as cookers, food mixers, microwave cookers, hair dryers, electric heaters and toasters. As most of the macrobiotic foods are alive, they are thought by macrobiotic practitioners to carry their own subtle form of living energy. This can be photographed by a process called Kirlian photography which was invented by a Russian scientist called Kirlian.

Although there is no scientific evidence of the effects of consistently cooking food within an electromagnetic field, from an electric cooker, macrobiotic cooks prefer the more natural methods of cooking and therefore predominantly use gas. For everyone with an electric cooker, changing to gas would incur considerable expense. However, whenever there is a choice, such as moving home or renovating a kitchen, I recommend gas cooker. In the meantime it does not help to worry about it.

1 William K. Stevens. New York Times, 1989

Much more important and something that warrants immediate attention is microwave cookers. They work by placing the food within a powerful electric field that induces the molecules within the food to move much faster than normal. This creates an increase in the temperature of the food and cooks it quickly. There are two issues. What happens to the food, and what happens to the people nearby? In the absence of any proper research I am convinced that cooking with a microwave cooker is an unnecessary risk. The effect of this electrical radiation on the living quality of the food is unknown, so why experiment on yourself. Secondly, all microwave cookers leak electrical radiation. The current discussion is what is a safe level. This is such a new subject that no-one can predict the long term effects on human health.

BODY

The skin covering our body provides the physical barrier between what is us and the outside world. We can eliminate unwanted substances from the body through the skin and even absorb substances through the skin. Oriental physicians made a strong connection between the skin, lungs and digestive system. They all have a similar function in that air does not really go inside the body until it is absorbed through the lining of the lungs. Otherwise the same air would be expelled. Similarly, food does not go inside the body until absorbed through the lining of the digestive system. So, just as clean fresh air improves the lungs, and healthy natural food improves the digestive system, so proper skin care will improve the function of the skin. Apart from looks, healthy skin will also contribute to overall health. Often the skin develops a layer of fat below the surface that reduces the skin's ability to 'breathe'. Check your own skin by taking a pinch on your forearm and roll it between finger and thumb. You can find differences from person to person. In addition see if you sweat from all over their body when ex ercising, have dryer skin or poorer circulation. All this indicates the health of the skin could be better. The following are some practical suggestions for skin care:

BODY SCRUBBING

Take a cotton face flannel, cotton nappy or small hand towel. Soak in hot water, wring out and vigorously scrub the skin everywhere from head till toe until red. Using a cloth rather than a loofah or brush which would be more abrasive, it is possible to apply more pressure and give the surface muscles a good massage. Thoroughly scrubbing the skin every day stimulates blood and lymph circulation. In addition, the scrubbing action has the effect of opening and closing the skin's pores effectively giving the skin a deep clean. To make the scrubbing even more effective, squeeze the juice from fresh grated ginger into water and heat up in a pan.

CREAMS, OILS

Eating a macrobiotic diet which is so low in saturated fat will help reduce the fat attached to skin, especially with regular scrubbing. However, if creams and oils are applied to the outside, the poor skin becomes sandwiched between two layers of fat, reducing its ability to breathe. Unless the skin is in strong sunlight, the body's own oil will keep the skin healthy and then it does not need oils. Once well established on a macrobiotic diet, with regular skin scrubbing, the skin usually improves naturally. Sometimes it could be a month between stopping the use of creams or oils before the skin's condition improves and during that time the skin might even become drier before it gets better. Dry skin can also be caused by soaps.

LONG HOT BATHS AND SAUNAS

During a long hot bath or sauna, the body sweats and loses salts and minerals. Although this is beneficial when the body needs to eliminate excess salts, if done too often it can lead to mineral deficiencies. If anyone feels dizzy when getting out of a hot bath, or feels tired after a bath or sauna, or has a history of mineral deficiencies, extra care is needed. I would recommend a short bath of 7 minutes or less just to get clean or a quick shower. Some people also add salts to their bath water to try and reduce the loss of minerals from the body.

CLOTHING

Because one of the basic principles of macrobiotics is the idea that anything living has its own living energy, and that this energy can be influenced, (for example by acupuncture) it is recommended that people wear clothing that does not carry a static charge. The idea being that synthetic clothing that carries a static charge would then effect the human's own natural energy. Most people find cotton clothing is easy to find and relatively inexpensive. Linen and silk would also be recommended. The most important are those materials that come into contact with the skin such as underwear, skirts, trousers, dresses, bed sheets, duvet covers, and pillow cases. I personally notice that, having not worn synthetic clothing for years, when I tried wearing nylon socks that my feet sweated more and my skin felt uncomfortable. Psychosomatic? Perhaps, but why not try it for yourself? I would also suggest that when at home, you take off your shoes and either wear soft shoes or just socks. This allows your feet to spread out and loosen up.

ELECTRICITY

Epidemiological studies by Nancy Wentheimer and Ed Leeper carried out in Denver U.S.A. on children who died of cancer between 1950 and 1973 found that children who lived near electrical distribution lines were twice as likely to develop cancer as those who did not. After much debate, a subsequent study commissioned by the New York State Power Lines Project confirmed the original findings. Since then, there has been much discussion and research into the effects of electromagnetic radiation from all sources, whether power-lines or household electrical appliances. Although it is too early to draw conclusions, the obvious message is that there is a potential risk. Those most at risk are pregnant women, where some research[2] has found a link

2 Kaiser-Permanente Medical Care Programme, Oakland, California, U.S.A., 1988

between electromagnetic radiation and miscarriages. I would therefore advise caution in the use of electrical appliances. Basically the less you use electrical appliances and the further you are from them the better. Exercise a sensible choice as to when and where you use them rather than be afraid to use them.

HOME AND WORK

The aim is to create a healthy atmosphere that naturally enhances the quality of life. Remember; macrobiotics literally means great life. So a successful work space will enhance concentration, creativity and productivity whereas qualities for a living space might be to enhance the ability to relax, play and socialise. A typical office, factory or home has changed a great deal in the last 50 years and it is worth looking at how some of these changes can effect our lives.

COMPUTERS and TV

Both the computer monitor and TV screen will emit electrical radiation. Some studies have shown an increased risk of breast cancer[3] and there is concern for pregnant women. However, this is disputed and so far not widely accepted. Macrobiotic practitioners are concerned that long-term exposure would adversely effect the nervous system as well as contribute to cancers effecting the periphery of the body. Fortunately the intensity of electrical radiation reduces logarithmically which means that sitting well away from a TV will make a significant difference. In addition, being selective and just watching programmes that you consider worth watching will reduce exposure. In the case of computer monitors, it is impossible to create a reasonable distance. However, even if the monitor is one metre away instead of a half metre, this makes a significant difference. In addition it is worth sitting to the side of the

3 Lancet Vol 3368730 page 1596, Dec 1990, and New York Academy of Sciences Vol 609, 1990

screen. A lead impregnated glass screen will also reduce radiation levels. I would finally suggest to anyone using a computer regularly that they turn off the screen whenever they are not using it. It is common to visit an office where all the screens are in operation but only a few people are using them at any one particular time.

FLUORESCENT LIGHTING

Many people find that this form of lighting increases the incidence of headaches and migraines. Whenever possible, I would suggest positioning yourself close to natural light. Use an incandescent light source rather than fluorescent.

FURNISHINGS

Choosing furnishings made of more natural materials will create a home or work space with a more living quality. Wood instead of plastic, wool carpets as opposed to nylon, or cotton fabrics to replace synthetics are all part of macrobiotic thinking. Again it must be emphasised that these concerns are applicable when someone is making a choice. If you already have a home that you wish to improve, do so by making the best choice, from what is available, each time something needs replacing. I personally find a space using predominantly natural materials much easier to relax in, more productive to work in and more comfortable.

PLANTS

A natural feel will again be enhanced by growing indoor plants. Not only do they look attractive but by bringing something alive into the home, you create a more natural quality.

LIFESTYLE

This is always personal and individual. Each person finds what they need to feel relaxed, energetic and healthy. For some, it may be yoga, for others competitive sports. For some it may be painting and for others sailing. For some it may be a challenging career, for others an active social life. Whatever it is, you can use it as a focus for your health. So you could eat in order to have the stamina to be an excellent athlete, to have the mental concentration to succeed in a particular career, or to have the creativity for a certain form of artistic expression. There are, however, some things that generally enhance your health.

This is trying to lead a balanced lifestyle. So if you like vigorous exercise, complement it with some relaxing stretches. If you lead a sedentary lifestyle, get some exercise. If your lifestyle is stressful, find ways to relax. In the same way any balanced exercise routine will include a variety of techniques. I always find it helpful to spend time in a park or in the countryside. For me, this provides a good balance to working indoors. I find it very relaxing, and at the same time invigorating. I particularly notice that after spending a few hours in a modern shopping centre how tired and mentally disoriented I feel, whereas I could spend all day walking in the countryside and still feel energetic and mentally alert.

Chapter 13

CHALLENGE AND CHANGE

by Simon Brown

For some people starting macrobiotics will be one of the biggest changes they will make in their lives. For most people, starting a macrobiotic diet involves making significant dietary changes. Sometimes people stop eating everything from their previous diet. When presented with a macrobiotic diet sheet I notice the look of amazement in friend's faces at what an enormous change this represents. It may be too much of a change for some people and the best they can do is to begin with those parts they can most readily introduce into their diet. However, anyone who fully takes on a macrobiotic diet and makes the biggest changes can expect to see the biggest results. If a health problem is the result of poor diet, the obvious action is to change the diet. The bigger the change in diet the bigger the potential improvement. It is often those people who eat the worst diets that have the most to gain. At the same time someone who eats a generally healthy diet will find it relatively easy to adapt to their new macrobiotic foods.

When starting it is always important to have a clear set of priorities. If you can identify what is most important to you, what makes life 'great' (macrobiotic) or important to you and then use macrobiotic foods to improve that. For Hugh Faulkner getting better was his main priority; other things came second to that. So given the choice of eating ice cream or his macrobiotic food, the choice would be made on the basis of whether that food would improve his health or not. This single minded approach is important for achieving the greatest success with macrobiotics. Your priority could be anything. If your dream is to win a marathon, then any time you have a choice of what to eat, that choice is made on the basis of whether it will improve your ability to win a marathon. Often good health will be the first priority when initially eating macrobiotically. However, that may be achieved relatively quickly as Hugh Faulkner found. After that, a bigger dream, ambition or goal is needed to establish a priority for life. Hugh Faulkner, at the age of 79 years old is still taking on new projects. For him, macrobiotics is worth the extra effort if the ability to do these things is the pay-off. For myself, the choices I make when deciding what to eat are based on the priorities I have in my life - to do my job well and take care of my family. For both of these I need a clear, focussed mind, physical vitality and the ability to cope with stress. My experience has been that careful attention to what I eat enhances my abilities to live up to my commitments.

In the end I think the following characteristics will give anyone a head-start - a spirit of adventure, a positive attitude, and a sense of humour. There is no doubt that eating macrobiotically is an adventure. It is an adventure that from time to time requires a degree of persistence and willpower. This is much easier when thinking positively about yourself and the opportunities to introduce positive changes. Finally, a sense of humour goes a long way.

Chapter 14

SHOPPING LISTS

by Simon Brown

When shopping, try to buy foods as close to their natural whole fresh condition as possible. whenever there is a choice, organic vegetables are always preferable. However, a wide variety of ingredients whether organic or not, is more important than being limited to a small range of organic foods. It is well worth asking your local health food shop to order any foods you cannot buy locally. Check labels for added sugar, the use of fats and additives in processed foods.

The following are available from most natural health food shops, some supermarkets or grocers:

GRAINS

Short grain brown rice
Barley
Millet
Jumbo oat flakes
Whole wheat noodles
Natural rise, sourdough or unyeasted bread
Couscous
Whole oats

Later use:
Wheat berries
Buckwheat
Rye
Quinoa

VEGETABLES

ROOTS

Carrots
Parsnips
Daikon /mooli
Swede
Radish
Turnip

GROUND

Pumpkin
Onion
Savoy Cabbage
Broccoli
Brussels Sprouts
Cauliflower
Red Cabbage

GREENS
- Leeks
- Spring onions
- Spring greens
- Kale
- Watercress
- Parsley
- Chinese leaf
- Lettuce

DRIED BEANS
- Aduki
- Brown lentils
- Chickpeas

Later use:
- Black-eyed beans
- Kidney beans
- Lima beans
- Pinto beans
- Soybeans
- Split peas

BEAN PRODUCTS
- Tofu
- Hummus

FISH
- Ideally wild fresh water fish or fresh deep sea fish from a fishmongers.

FRUIT
- Apples
- Pears
- Strawberries
- Raspberries
- Melon
- Grapes
- Blackcurrants
- Plums
- Blackberries
- Apricots
- Peaches
- Nectarines
- Raisins
- Cherries
- Tangerines

RAW NUTS
- Peanuts
- Walnut
- Hazelnuts
- Almonds
- Dried chestnuts

RAW SEEDS
- Sesame
- Sunflower
- Pumpkin

DRINKS
- Fruit juice (see list of fruits) - apple
- Spring water
- Real ales or Guinness
- Grain coffee
- Dandelion coffee
- Chamomile tea
- Fresh carrot juice
- Homemade vegetable juice

SWEETENERS
- Barley malt or malt extract

SEASONINGS
- Unrefined white sea salt
- Ginger
- Lemon
- Garlic
- Mustard

OILS
- Cold-pressed sesame oil, sunflower oil, corn oil, safflower oil

SPREADS
- Peanut butter
- Sesame butter
- Tahini
- Sugar free jams

PICKLES
- Natural sauerkraut
- Natural gherkins

SPECIALITY MACROBIOTIC INGREDIENTS

The following are more unusual macrobiotic ingredients that are found in the larger or specialist health food shops. They may also be ordered by mail-order from Clearspring Natural foods. (see Useful Addresses)

SEAWEEDS
- Wakame
- Kombu
- Arame
- Hiziki
- Dulse
- Nori
- Agar-agar (kanten)

DRINKS
- Loose Bancha tea
- Yannoh (coffee substitute)

SWEETENERS
- Brown rice syrup
- Amazake

SOYA PRODUCTS
- Tempeh (usually comes frozen)
- Natto (usually comes frozen)

OPTIONAL PROCESSED FOODS
- Seitan
- Fu
- Dried tofu

SEASONINGS
- Umeboshi plums
- Kuzu
- Umeboshi vinegar
- Brown rice vinegar
- Barley
- Miso
- Shoyu (natural soya sauce)
- Shiso sprinkle
- Tekka

OPTIONAL GRAINS
- Mochi
- Hatto mugi
- Udon noodles
- Soba noodles

MACROBIOTIC CONVENIENCE FOODS

Although not always recommended it is helpful to be familiar with macrobiotic convenience foods for emergencies, travelling or quick snacks.

There are now a wide range of convenience foods not listed such as sugar, honey and carob free sweets, tofu burgers etc.

GRAINS
- Mochi
- 5 minute noodles and powdered sauce
- Wholemeal pitta bread
- Sugar-free wheatflakes or cornflakes
- Sugar-free muesli

BISCUITS
- Sugar-free digestive biscuits or cookies
- Rice cakes
- Oat cakes

BEAN PRODUCTS
- Smoked tofu
- Hummus

DRINKS
- Bancha tea bags

SEASONINGS / SAUCES / SPREADS
- Vegan pesto sauce
- Tofu spreads
- Peanut butter
- Sesame butter
- Tahini (best from roasted seeds)
- Instant miso soup

VEGETABLES
- Sauerkraut
- Raw vegetables

EATING OUT

- Salads - vegetable, pasta, bean
- Fish and vegetables
- Spaghetti and vegetables, or seafood sauce
- Hummus pitta and salads
- Lentil soups
- Fruit salad

Chapter 15

THE OLDER THE BOLDER

by Hugh Faulkner

Granny learned to dance at eighty-two,
A really odd type thing to do,
And when she'd learned both tap and ballet,
She changed her name from Maud to Sally.

She said: "Till now I've done things right,
I've never stayed up all the night,
Or learned a great magician's trick,
Or eaten cake until I'm sick.

I was too busy, don't you see,
To ever really just be me."

Nanette Newman - "My Granny"
quoted by Bernice Martin

After I began to believe that my cancer was in remission, I realised that I felt fitter and more full of energy than I had for years. If this was the result of the macrobiotic diet and life-style, could it help others of my age who didn't have cancer? Further, without the threat of a death sentence, would any of my fellow senior citizens be prepared to change the habits of a life time?

Many years ago, I heard of a club started by the novelist C. R. Nevinson called "The Older the Bolder". I never knew any details, but I believe the club organised adventure holidays for older people, and the name stayed in my mind. Looking back over my patients, relatives and friends I realised that old people fall roughly into two categories, those who see old age as a threat and those who see it as a challenge. Why is there such an enormous difference between different people of the same age? Why do some people lose their autonomy and independence and others not?

This is the area our research project seeks to explore. Shortly before my illness our health district which covers six communes of the Chianti zone, planned research into the relative risk of the factors involved in the loss of autosufficiency in old people in the area. In the first phase we intend to organise meetings of small groups of old people in two of our communes - one truly rural and one closer to Florence and more urban.

Our project is based on a number of hypotheses - for example that each individual is unique, that there are probably major differences between old people in different settings, and that old people themselves may provide information in small groups that has not emerged in the many traditional questionaires which have been carried out in several places. We have been promised funding for our pilot survey by the EEC, and now seek further finance to complete the project.

In the past 200 years the demographic profile of most countries, including Britain, has been completely transformed.[1]

Instead of populations consisting mainly of young adults and children, in Britain one third of the population is now over the age of 50 and nearly a fifth over 60. On average girls born in 1986 can expect to live to the age of 78 - six years longer than their brothers. This change s mainly due to decreases in the birth-rate and death-rate. Both have many causes. Curative medicine may have played a part in prolonging life and vaccination has helped to reduce the incidence of the killer infections of childhood, but the death-rate had begun to decline long before these became

1 Jefferys, M. from *Aspects of Aging*. Editors Bury and Macnicol (see book list)

widely available, and appears to be due mainly to improved diet and living and working conditions. We can expect the death-rate at all ages to decrease steadily in the last decade of the millenium. In 1981 only 11 in each 1000 of the population in Britain were ages 85 or more, but by the year 2001 some 17 in each 1000 will be 85 or older. Inevitably those over 85 are more likely to become dependent on care, but as Prof. Jeffreys points out "A technologically innovative and ingenious society such as ours ought to be able to sustain such a proportion of dependents even if they were all - as they clearly are not - in need of tending day in and day out". However this won't happen automatically, and the community services for the elderly today are far from universally adequate, and vary greatly from place to place, and country to country.

We have a great deal of information about prevention of disease and disability in old age which is not being acted upon - either by local authorities or by old people themselves. There are many popular misconceptions about old people, and one of the most widely held is that illness is synonymous with old age. In fact many of us are fully active and independent, and our numbers should increase if we switch to a healthier diet and life-style. Here too orthodox curative medicine has made major contributions in such fields as hip replacement and cardiac surgery, and has given many old people a new lease of life, and restored their autonomy and independence.

In our region of Italy, we estimate that nearly a quarter of the population will be over 65 by the year 2000, and the proportion of voters over 65 will obviously be even greater. This opens up the obvious opportunity to create an effective lobby for more adequate pensions, housing and community services for old people. What government, local authority or political party could possibly afford to ignore the demands of over a quarter of their voters? The pensioners' trade unions and some of the voluntary organisations are well aware of this, but relatively few old people seem to be actively involved.

In the book *"Aspects of Aging"*, Bernice Martin suggests that we are in the midst of a major revision of society's attitude to old age at the present time. There is a growing number of four generation families, but in Britain, relatively few are in old people's homes, and the majority live independently. For manual workers - at any rate since the industrial revolution - old age is synonymous with poverty.

In Britain in the 1980's, 70% of the retired population relied on their state pension - the lowest in the Common Market - for their only source of income. Poverty and the illusion of powerlessness have been the hallmarks of old age for most workers.

We do not know how long we can live if we adopt a healthy diet and life-style. As far as I know no one has yet organised a long-term trial of longevity in macrobiotics, and apart from Michio and Aveline Kushi, most of the followers of macrobiotics we have met have carried out the diet and life-style for less than 20 years, and have not yet entered the ranks of the third age. There have recently been forecasts in the press of life spans of 110, 120 and even 130 years, but these seem to have met with little general credence amongst scientists.

Susan Sontag has described the ways in which women are penalised in old age. It is much more important for a woman to feel desirable and preserve her physical appearance, than for a man. Aging tends to unsex women, whereas men can claim to be attractive for longer, especially if they possess the added advantages of money or power. The popularity of beauty care for those women who can afford it, and the fact that more men than women remarry after divorce, testify to this sex difference. Moreover women live longer than men and they are still expected to care for aged relatives -often at a time when their own children have grown up and they could reasonably expect some leisure time for themselves.

There are dangers in this frantic search for eternal youth. Clearly few women are going to be able to compete with retired film-stars, and even with the help of macrobiotics we are not all likely to enjoy a second adolescence. If we fail to make it, we may be accused of not trying hard enough - the old game of "blaming the victim". Of course some people have managed to retain their beauty, energy and creativity well into the third age. But these are as exceptional as the young people who win open tennis tournaments and swimming championships in their early teens.

The attitude of society to old age has changed fundamentally, certainly in the United States and Western Europe. The image of old people as passive, helpless, unimportant, uninteresting and dreary, is fading fast. There are many reasons for this, and here I can only touch on one or two. Some 90% of all non-manual workers in the United States are now said to enjoy the benefits of occupational or private pension insurance schemes. Marketing firms have not failed to recognise a potential new market here, and the travel firm Argosy, which specialises in providing holidays for the older age group, is apparently highly successful. Edwina Currie, a previous junior Minister of Health, with a knack for the infelicitous phrase, speaks of the "Woopy" - the well-off old person.

In the cinema, television and even detective stories, old people emerge as powerful personalities - and in the case of Monty Python's "Hell's Grannies" - even violent. In Agatha Christie's novels Miss Marple solves murders seated in her cottage in a peaceful English village; Compo and his mates pull off all the tricks in "The Last of the Summer Wine"; Clive Dunn in "Dad's Army" frequently gets the better of his commanding officer. Figures of fun, yes - but far removed from the old biddies of the seaside postcards and Shakespeare's slippered pantaloon, shuffling to the grave.

Those of us already old - or even 'old old' - are faced with a choice. We can either settle for a passive role, beset by fears of loss of status, loss of memory, vision, hearing or incapacitating disability and, for most of us, fear of poverty; or we can decide to take the initiative - to be bold. So where can we be bold? First, the enjoyment of leisure and retirement demands adequate financing. Today, in most western countries there are many old people below the poverty line. This is clearly unacceptable. By leaving paid employment we have not left society, which is still responsible for us.

At one of our Chianti workshops for old people, one participant said that the key question for him was freedom to choose, and that this implied an adequate income. We have to be able to decide whether we want to go on working, either full or part-time, where work exists. We must be free to choose whether to enter contributory state or private pension schemes. Here we need objective accurate information and advice, and the pensioners' trade unions and voluntary bodies will have to provide experts in this complex field, and fully inform themselves.

We need a powerful lobby at the national and EEC level, where many of the decisions affecting old people will be made in coming years. We need to lobby all political parties, and play an active role in the pensioners' trade unions and old people's organizations. We have to emerge from our isolation and helplessness and discover our potential strength.

At local authority level much remains to be done. There are enormous differences in the provisions for old people's housing, health and social services, and leisure facilities in the countries we know best - and in different areas within each country. It is too soon to say whether the new provisions in general practice in Britain will help or hinder the health care of old people. A great deal is known about preventive measures in the community in old age and we have to insist that all local authority services rise to the level of the best. Space does not allow us to go into details on this subject here, but we are preparing a book which will inform our fellow senior citizens on what they can do, and supply them with ammunition for the battles ahead.

How can we ourselves to bold? First, we can respond to the opportunities presented by the present climate of opinion. Everywhere authoritarianism is being rejected, men and women are demanding liberty, and the old can break their chains. We are all individuals, with the capacity to change and grow at almost any age. We all have enormous resources - for the most part unused. Old age can become a time for adventure, when we cheerfully go out to meet new challenges. To be able to do this we need to be as fit as possible. We need to look at our diet and our way of life. We believe a macrobiotic diet can make us healthier in old age, can improve the quality of our lives and perhaps help us to live longer. But even if we are not all prepared to embark on the macrobiotic path, there is plenty of evidence from orthodox dieticians that old people do better on less animal fat, less refined salt and sugar, few if any cigarettes and little alcohol, and with more grains and vegetables. When we retire we tend to sit around more, when in fact we need regular exercise to keep fit. This can take the form we prefer - walking, swimming, tennis, bowls, keep-fit exercises - what you will. One important thing is to enjoy it all, and not to try to break any records!

Lastly, all kinds of activity is good. Old age is a time for doing the things you've always wanted to do. You will be surprised how much energy you have. If you missed out on study and education the first time round, what about the 'University of the Third Age', local authority hobby and language classes, music and acting? Never were there so many opportunities. We can make sure our minority interests are catered for. Never was there a better time for old people to be bold! It's up to us to see we have the right to spend our old age in the way we choose.

BOOK LIST

These are some of the books and articles we have read in preparing this book. They are in alphabetical order according to the surname of the first author.

Achterberg, Jeanne. "Imagery in Healing: Shamanism and Modern Medicine" New Science Library (Shambhala) Boston and London 1985.

Alexander, F. Matthias. "Constructive Conscious Control of the Individual" Integral Press UK 1955.

Al Huang, Chungliang. "Embrace Tiger, Return to Mountain" (The Essence of Tai Ji) Celestial Arts Berkeley, California 1987.

Altschuler, S. "Dietary Protein and Calcium Loss: A Review" Nutritional Research 2: 193 1982.

Anderson, E. and Anderson, P. "General Practitioners and Alternative Medicine" Journal R.C.G.P. London February 1987.

Andreas, Connirae and Steve. "Heart of the Mind" Real People Press 1989.

Asher, J. J. "Brainswitching" Sky Oakes Productions USA 1985.

Assagioli, Roberto. "Psychosynthesis" Turnstone Press Limited UK 1975.

Bach, E. "The Medical Discoveries" C. W. Daniel Rochford, England 1940.

Balitsky, K. P. et al. "Some Electro-physical Peculiarities of the Nervous System in Malignant Growth" Annals of the N.Y. Academy of Science N.164, 520-5. 1969.

Bandler, Richard. "Using your Brain for a Change" Real People Press USA 1985.

Bandler, Richard and Grinder, John. "Frogs into Princes" (Neurolinguistic Programming) Real People Press USA 1979.

Bandler, Richard and Grinder, John. "Reframing" (Neurolinguistic Programming and the Transformation of Meaning) Real People Press Moab Utah 1982.
Barborka, Geoffrey A. "The Divine Plan" Theosophical Publishing House Madras India 1964.
Barlow, Wilfred. "The Alexander Principle" Victor Gollancz London 1973.
Benedict, Dirk. "Confessions of a Kamikaze Cowboy" Newcastle Publishing co. Inc. California 1987.
Benjamin, Harry. "Better Sight Without Glasses" Health For All Publishing Co. UK 1944.
Bohm, D. "Causality and Chance in Modern Physics" Routledge and Kegan Paul London 1984.
Booth, Roger "Psychoneuroimmunology" Caduceus (published quarterly) Winter, 1990 p.28.
du Boulay, Shirley. "Cicely Saunders" Hodder and Stoughton UK 1984.
Bowler, Jane. Editor of: "The Vegetarian Travel Guide" The Vegetarian Society 1991.
Brady, Kate and Considine, Mike. "The London Guide to Mind Body and Spirit" Brainwave London UK 1988.
Brohn, Penny. "The Bristol Programme" Century Paperbacks UK 1987.
Brown, Simon. "Vital Touch" Community Health Foundation. London 1991.
Burk, J. "The Day the Universe Changed" BBC London 1985.
Bury, Michael and Macnicol, John (Editors). "Aspects of Aging" Essays on Social Policy and Old Age. Social Policy Papers No. 3 England 1990.
Cameron-Bandler, L., Gordin, D. and Lebean, M. "The Emprint Method" Future Pace USA 1985.
Cameron-Bandler, L. "Solutions" Future Pace USA 1985.
Campbell, Giraud W. "A Doctor's Proven New Home Cure for Arthritis" Thorsons England 1979.
Cannon, Geoffrey. "The Politics of Food" Century London 1987.
Capra, F. "Uncommon Wisdom" Rider London 1985.
Carlson, Richard and Shield, Benjamin (Editors) "Healers on Healing" Jeremy Tarcher Inc. Los Angeles 1989.

Chang, Edward C. "Knocking at the Gate of Life" Thorsons/Rodale UK 1986.
Cheng, Man-ch'ing "T'ai Chi Ch'uan" (A Simplified Method of Calisthenics for Health and Self Defense) North Atlantic Books Berkeley California 1981.
Chia, Mantak and Chia, Maneewan "Cultivating Female Sexual Energy" Healing Tao Books New York 1986.
Chia, Mantak. "Awaken Healing Energy through the Tao" Aurora Press New York 1984.
Chia, Mantak and Winn, Michael. "Taoist Secrets of Love: Cultivating Male Sexual Energy" Aurora Press New York 1984.
Chichester, F. "How to Keep Fit" Hodder and Stoughton London 1969.
Chopra, Deepak. "Quantum Healing" Bantam Books London 1989.
Clyne, Rachel. "Coping with Cancer: Making Sense of it all" Thorsons Publishing Group New York 1986.
Comerford, John. "Health the Unknown - the Story of the Peckham Experiment" Hamish Hamilton London 1947.
Comfort, Alex. "A Good Age" Mitchell Beazley London 1977.
Cousins, Norman. "Head First - The Biology of Hope" E. P. Dutton USA 1989.
Cousins, Norman. "Anatomy of an Illness - as perceived by the patient" Bantam Books Inc. New York USA 1989.
Coward, Rosalind "The Whole Truth" Faber and Faber London 1989.
Cowmeadow, Oliver. "An Introduction to Macrobiotics" Thorsons Publ. Group 1987.
Davies, P. "Other Worlds" Dent UK 1980.
Dawkins, Richard. "The Blind Watchmaker" Penguin Books 1988.
Doll, Sir Richard. Harveian Oration 1982. Quoted by Geoffrey Cannon. "The Politics of Food" Century Paperback London 1987.
Dominique, Rosel. "Il Cucchiaio de Legno" Edizione Probios Firenze 1986.

Donden, Yeshi. "Health Through Balance: An Introduction to Tibetan Medicine" Snow Lion Publications Ithaca New York USA 1986.

Dossey, Larry. "Space, Time and Medicine" New Science Library (Shambhala) Boston and London 1982.

Dossey, Larry. "Beyond Illness" New Science Library (Shambhala) USA 1984.

Downie, Patricia. "Cancer Rehabilitation" Faber and Faber London 1978.

Downing, George. "The Massage Book" Penguin Books 1983.

Doyal, Lesley and Epstein, Samuel S. "Cancer in Britain" Pluto Press London 1983.

Doyal, Lesley and Pennell, Imogen. "The Political Economy of Health" Pluto Press London 1979.

Dufty, William. "Sugar Blues - Il Mal de Zucchero" Macro/edizione Italy 1987.

Duncan, R. and Weston-Smith, M. "The Encyclopedia of Ignorance" Pergamon Press UK 1977.

Eccles, J. C. "The Human Mystery" Routledge and Kegan Paul London 1984.

Editorial: "Alternative Medicine" British Medical Journal Vol. 287 No. 6388 1983.

Editorial: "What Kind of Alternative is Alternative Medicine?" Journal RCGP N.35 459-461 1985.

Edwards, Phil. and Totah, Hilary. "Heart to Hara" The Rebirth and Creative Birth Centre UK 1987.

Egan, Gerard. "The Skilled Helper" Brooks/Cole Publishing Company California 1986.

Ehrenreich, John. "The Cultural Crisis of Modern Medicine" Monthly Review Press New York and London 1978.

Eisenberg, D. and Wright, T. L. "Encounters with Ki: Exploring Chinese Medicine" Norton New York 1985.

Esko, Edward (Editor) "Doctors Look at Macrobiotics" Japan Publications Inc. Tokyo and New York 1988.

Estelle, Mary. "Natural Foods Cookbook - Vegetarian Dairy-Free Cuisine" Japan Publications Inc. Tokyo and New York 1985.

Ferruci, P. "Crescere" Astrolabio Roma 1981.
Fisher, Roger and Ury, William. "Getting to Yes" Hutchinson Business UK 1981.
Forbes, Alec. "The Bristol Diet" Century Arrow UK 1986.
Fox, William W. "Arthritis and Allied Conditions" Published privately, printed at the Raneleigh Press London 1975.
Friedman, Meyer and Rosenmann. "Type A Behaviour and Your Heart" Knopf New York 1974.
Gate, Gabriel. "Family Food" Anne O'Donovan Pty. Ltd. Victoria Australia 1987.
Gawler, Ian. "You can Conquer Cancer" Hill of Content Melbourne 1984.
Glouberman, Dina. "Life Choices and Life Changes through Imagework" Unwin Hyman London 1989.
Gould, J. L. and C. G. "Life at the Edge" W. H. Freeman, New York 1989.
Griggs, Barbara. "The Food Factor" Penguin Books London 1988.
Grinder, John and DeLozier, Judith. "Turtles All The Way Down: Prerequisites for Personal Genius" Grinder, Delozier and Associates, California 1987.
Hafen, Brent and Frandsen, Kathryn. "An A-Z of Alternative Medicine" Sheldon Press London 1984.
Haley, Jay "Uncommon Therapy - the Psychiatric Techniques of Milton H. Erickson, M.D." W. W. Norton New York and London 1986.
Harrison, John. "Love your Disease - it's Keeping you Healthy" Angus and Robertson London 1984.
Haslett, Peter. "A Fresh May of Life" Weidenfield Nicolson UK 1989.
Hausman, P. "Jack Sprat's Legacy - the Science and Politics of Fat and Cholesterol" Richard Mank New York 1981.
Hay, Louise. "You can Heal your Life" Hay House UK 1984.
Heidenry, Carolyn. "Making the Transition to a Macrobiotic Diet" Avery Wayne New Jersey USA 1984.
Hindhede, Mikkel. "The Effect of Food Restrictions during War - on Mortality in Copenhagen" Journal American Medical Association 74 (6): 381 1920.

Hodgkinson, Neville. "Will to be Well" Hutchinson London 1984.

Hoffman, David. "The Holistic Herbal" Element Books UK 1989.

Hovnanian, Ralph R. "Medical Dark Ages Circa 1984" Published by Author Evanston Ill. USA 1985.

Humphreys, Christmas. "The Wisdom of Buddhism" Michael Joseph London 1960.

Iliffe, Steve. "The NHS A Picture of Health" Lawrence and Wishart London 1983.

Illich, Ivan. "Limits to Medicine" Penguin Books 1977.

Irwin, Yukiko and Wagenvoord, James. "Shiatzu" Routledge and Kegan Paul London 1977.

Johnson, N. et al. "Effect of Level of Protein Intake on Urinary and Fecal Calcium Retention" Journal of Nutrition: 100: 1425 1970.

Kaptchuk, Ted J. "Chinese Medicine - The Web that has no Weaver" Rider London 1983.

Kennedy, Ian. "The Unmasking of Medicine" Granada London 1983.

Kennett, Frances. "Folk Medicine Fact or Fiction" Marshall Cavendish London 1984.

Kenyon, Julian N. "21st Century Medicine - A Layman's Guide to the Medicine of the Future" Thorsons Publishers England 1986.

Kidman, Brenda. "A Gentle Way With Cancer" Century Arrow London 1986.

Kotzsch, Ronald E. "Macrobiotics Yesterday and Today" Japan Publications Inc. Tokyo and New York 1985.

Kushi, Aveline with Jack, Alex. "Complete Guide to Macrobiotic Cooking for Health, Harmony and Peace" Warner Books New York 1985.

Kushi, Aveline and Esko, Wendy. "Aveline Kushi's Wonderful World of Salads" Japan Publications Inc. Tokyo and New York 1980.

Kushi, Michio. "The Book of Do-In - Exercises for Physical and Spiritual Development" Japan Publications Inc.

Kushi, Michio. "How to see your Health: the Book of Oriental Diagnosis" Japan Publications Inc. Tokyo and New York 1980.

Kushi, Michio and Cottrell, Martha with Mead, Mark N. "Aids, Macrobiotics and Natural Immunity" Japan Publication Inc. Tokyo and New York 1990.

Kushi, Michio with Jack, Alex. "The Cancer Prevention Diet. Thorsons Wellingborough 1984.

Lang, S. "Diet and Disease" Food Monitor p.244 May/June 1983.

Ledvinka, Ferro. "Macrobiotica: Consigli Pratici per Chi Inizia" Pianeta Terra Firenze Italy 1986.

Levenson, Frederick B. "The Causes and Prevention of Cancer" Sidgwick and Jackson London 1985

Levin, D. M. and Soloman, G. G. non-dated paper distributed at The Esalen Institute, Esalen, California: The Discursive Formation of the Body in the History of Medicine.

Levins, Richard and Lewontin, Richard. "The Dialectical Biologist" Harvard University Press Cambridge Massachusetts 1985.

Levitt, Paul M. and Guralnick, Elissa S. "The Cancer Reference Book" Harper and Row London 1984.

Lewith, George T. and Kenyon, Julian N. "Clinical Ecology: The Treatment of Ill-health Caused by Environmental Factors" Thorsons Wellingborough 1985.

Mackenzie, W. J. M. "Power and Responsibility in Health Care" Oxford University Press UK 1979.

Manning, Matthew. "Guide to Self Healing" Thorsons Wellingborough UK 1989.

Maultsby, Maxie C. "Help Yourself to Happiness - through Rational Self- Counselling" Institute for Rational-Emotive Therapy New York 1975.

McCarty, Meredith. "American Macrobiotic Cuisine" Turning Point Publications California 1986.

Mintz, Sidney W. "Sweetness and Power - the Place of Sugar in Modern History" Penguin Books London 1986.

Mitchell, Keith. "The Practically Macrobiotic Cookbook" Thorsons Wellingborough 1987.

Nussbaum, Elaine. "Recovery - From Cancer to Health Through Macrobiotics" Japan Publications Tokyo and New York 1985.

Ohsawa, George. "Macrobiotics, The Way of Healing" George Ohsawa Macrobiotic Foundation California 1984.

Ohsawa, George. "Zen Macrobiotics - the Art of Rejuvenation and Longevity" The Ohsawa Foundation Inc. California 1965.

Oldfield, Harry and Coghill, Roger. "The Dark Side of the Brain" Element Books England 1988.

Ots, Thomas. "The Angry Liver, the Anxious Heart and the Melancholy Spleen" Culture, Medicine and Psychiatry 114: 21-58 1990.

Paroni, Elisabetta. "Macrobiotica in Cucina" La Cas Verde Italy 1989.

Pearce, Ian C. B. "The Holistic Approach to Cancer" R. Findlay Scotland 1983.

Pelletier, Kenneth R. "Mind as Healer Mind as Slayer - A Holistic approach to Preventing Stress Disorders" A Delta Book Del Publishing Co. Inc. New York 1977.

Pietroni, Patrick. "The Greening of Medicine" Victor Gollancz London 1990.

Porkert, Manfred. "The Theoretical Foundations of Chinese Medicine" The Massachusetts Institute of Technology USA 1985.

Purucker, G. de. "Wind of the Spirit" Point Loma Publications Inc. California 1971.

Ray, Sandra. "I Deserve Love" (How Affirmations Can Guide You to Personal Fulfillment) Celestial Arts Berkeley California 1976.

Ridolfi, Ray. "Shiatsu" Optima London 1990.

Robbins, Anthony. "Unlimited Power" (The New Science of Personal Achievement) Simon and Schuster UK 1988.

Robbins, John. "Diet for a New America" Stillpoint Publishing Walpole USA 1987.

Rogers, Sherry. "The E.I. Syndrome" Prestige New York 1986.

Rogers, Sherry. "Tired or Toxic?" Prestige Publishing New York 1990.

Rogers, Sherry. "You Are What You Ate" Prestige New York 1988.

Salmon, J. Warren. "Alternative Medicine" Tavistock Publications New York and London 1985.

Sams, Craig. "About Macrobiotics - The Way of Eating" Thorsons Wellingborough UK 1985.

Sattilaro, Anthony J. "Recalled by Life" Avon Books New York 1982.

Schneider, Meir. "Self-Healing - My Life and Vision" Arkana London 1989.

Scott, Jimmy with Goss, Kathleen. "Cure Your Own Allergies in Minutes" Health Kinesiology Publications San Francisco 1988.

Sidman, Murray. "Coercion and its Fallout" Authors Cooperative Inc. Publishers Boston Mass. 1989.

Steiner, Rudolf and Wegman, Itma. "Fundamentals of Therapy" Rudolf Steiner Press London 1985.

Strom, A and Jensen, R. A. "Mortality from Circulatory Diseases in Norway 1940-1945" Lancet 260: p.126-129 1951.

Turner, Gordon. "A Time to Heal" Corgi Book (Transworld Publishers Ltd.) UK 1974.

Turner, Roger Newman. "Naturopathic Medicine" Thorsons Wellingborough UK 1985.

Walford, R. "Maximum Life Span" Norton London 1983.

Watkins, Steve. "Medicine and Labour - The Politics of a Profession" Lawrence and Wishart London 1987.

Weber, Marcea. "Wholemeals" Prism Press Dorset UK 1983.

Wright, Beric. "Ease and Dis-Ease" Longman Professional London 1986.

Yudkin, John. "The Penguin Encyclopedia of Nutrition" Penguin Books UK 1986.

USEFUL ADDRESSES FOR EDUCATIONAL CENTRES

GREAT BRITAIN
Community Health
Foundation
188 Old Street
London EC1V 9FR
Phone: 071-251 4076

U.S.A.
Kushi Institute
Box 7, Becket, Mass.01223
U.S.A.
Phone 413 623 5742

Vega Study Center
1511 Robinson Street
Oroville, California 95965
U.S.A.
Phone 916 553 7702

International Macrobiotic
Shiatsu Society
1122 M Street
Eureka, CA95501-2442
U.S.A.
Phone 707 445 2290

SWITZERLAND
I.M.I.
Kientalerhof
CH-3723, Kiental
Switzerland
Phone 33 76 2676

HOLLAND
Kushi Institute
65 Weteringschaus
1017RX
Amsterdam, Holland
Phone: 20257513

BELGIUM
Antwerp East West Centre
Consciencestraate 44
Belgium 2018 Antwerp

SPAIN
Instituto Cosmobiotico
De Espana
Anselem Clave
3 bis. 08190 Sant Cugat
Del Valles
Barcelona, Spain
Phone 93 589 12 69

PORTUGAL
Instituto Macropbiotico
De Portugal
Rua Dos Correeiros 14
Portugal 1200 Lisboa
Phone 1342-6551

GERMANY
Makropbiotik in Berlin e.V.
z.Hd. Hans Schmidt
Schustherusstr.26
1000 Berlin 10
Phone 030 341 2888/
030 341 4166

USEFUL ADDRESSES FOR SHOPS IN GREAT BRITAIN

Clearspring Wholefoods
196 Old Street, London EC1V 9BP
Phone 071-250 1708

Clearspring distribute a full range of macrobiotic foods to health food shops throughout the U.K. For details of the nearest shop to you call 081-749 1781.

MAIL ORDER
Clearspring Wholefoods
Phone 081-746 2261

INDEX

CHF MAIL ORDER

■ *BOOKS*

'VITAL TOUCH',
Simon Brown & Dan Fletcher.
Softback. £4.95 + £1.00 p&p.

Vital Touch is a unique exercise programme deriving from the ancient oriental art of *Do-In*. *Do-In* means literally 'self massage' and involves the stimulation of special acupressure points.

Now available for the first time as a series of practical, easy-to-follow illustrations with notes, these exercises are simple to learn and need very little space. Ideal for toning up, invigorating or relaxing the mind and body.

A CHF Publication.

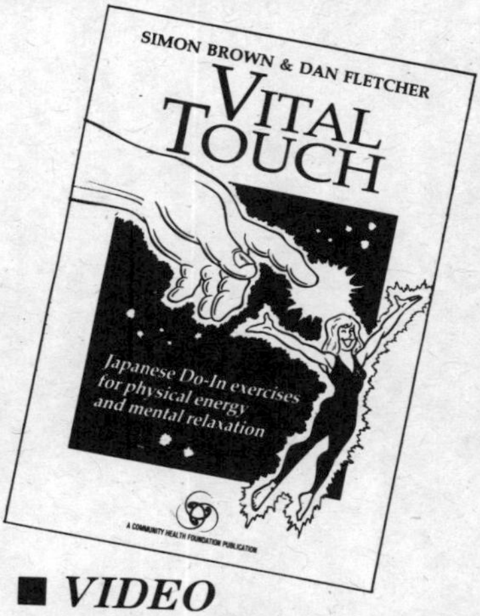

'GETTING WELL AGAIN',
Drs Simonton.
Softback. £5.99 + £1.00 p&p.

An uplifting, inspiring and life affirming book outlining their extraordinary work with helping terminal cancer patients to improve their quality of life and often live years longer than the official prognosis.

'CANCER PREVENTION DIET',
Michio Kushi.
Softback. £4.99 + £1.00 p&p.

The comprehensive and seminal text for anyone interested in improving their health or worried out their present condition.

■ *VIDEO*

'AN INTRODUCTION TO MACROBIOTICS'
Keith Michell and the CHF teaching staff.
40 mins VHS. £9.95 + £1.00 p&p.

An interesting, informative and easy to understand guide to Macrobiotics explaining the basic Eastern principles and also the latest Western confirmation of this health giving diet.

A CHF Production.

All of the above items are available from: CHF Mail Order, The Community Health Foundation, 188 Old St., London EC1V 9FR. Please enclose cheque/PO for the appropriate remittance with postage. We accept Visa and Mastercard. Please quote the relevant number and expiry date.
Enquiries on 071-251 4076.